ALIA'S MISSION

SAVING THE BOOKS OF IRAQ

Inspired by a True Story

Mark Alan Stamaty

Dragonfly Books ———— New York

For Janet Schulman

All rights reserved. Published in the United States by Dragonfly Books, an imprint of Random House Children's Books, a division of Random House, Inc., New York. Original published in hardcover in the United States by Alfred A. Knopf, an imprint of Random House Children's Books, a division of Random House, Inc., New York, in 2004.

Dragonfly Books with the colophon is a registered trademark of Random House, Inc.

Visit us on the Web! www.randomhouse.com/kids

Educators and librarians, for a variety of teaching tools, visit us at www.randomhouse.com/teachers

The Library of Congress has cataloged the hardcover edition of this work as follows:
Stamaty, Mark Alan.
Alia's mission: saving the books of Iraq / by Mark Alan Stamaty.
p.   cm.
ISBN 978-0-375-83217-8 (trade) — ISBN 978-0-375-93217-5 (lib. bdg.)
[1. Baker, Alia Muhammad—Juvenile literature. 2. Librarians—Iraq—Basrah—Biography—Juvenile literature. 3. Libraries—Iraq—Basrah—Juvenile literature. 4. Iraq War 2003—Destruction and pillage—Juvenile literature.] I. Title.
Z720.B24S73 2004   020'.92—dc22   2004048633

ISBN 978-0-375-85763-8 (pbk.)

MANUFACTURED IN CHINA

10 9 8 7 6 5 4 3 2 1

First Dragonfly Books Edition

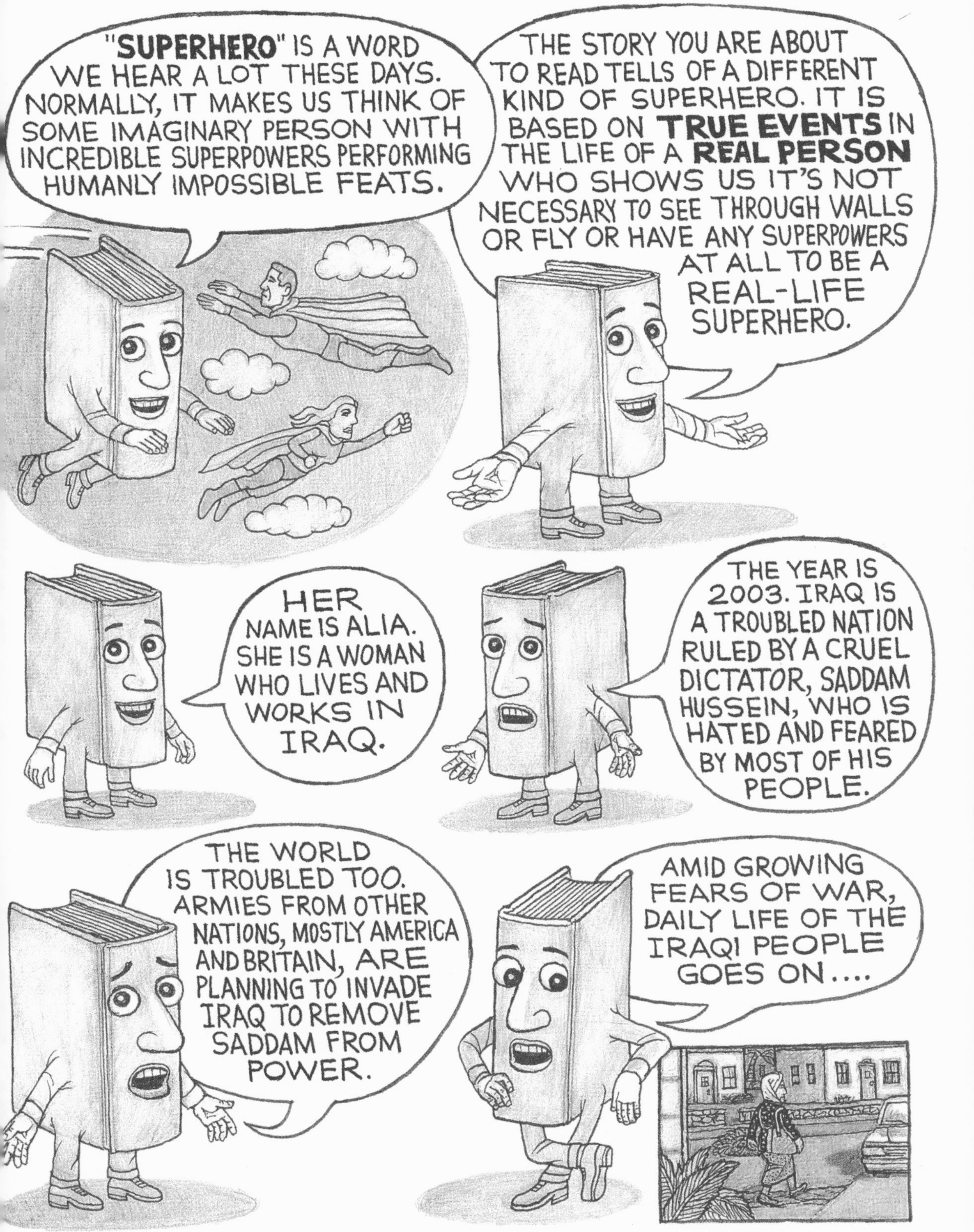
"SUPERHERO" IS A WORD WE HEAR A LOT THESE DAYS. NORMALLY, IT MAKES US THINK OF SOME IMAGINARY PERSON WITH INCREDIBLE SUPERPOWERS PERFORMING HUMANLY IMPOSSIBLE FEATS.
THE STORY YOU ARE ABOUT TO READ TELLS OF A DIFFERENT KIND OF SUPERHERO. IT IS BASED ON TRUE EVENTS IN THE LIFE OF A REAL PERSON WHO SHOWS US IT'S NOT NECESSARY TO SEE THROUGH WALLS OR FLY OR HAVE ANY SUPERPOWERS AT ALL TO BE A REAL-LIFE SUPERHERO.
HER NAME IS ALIA. SHE IS A WOMAN WHO LIVES AND WORKS IN IRAQ.
THE YEAR IS 2003. IRAQ IS A TROUBLED NATION RULED BY A CRUEL DICTATOR, SADDAM HUSSEIN, WHO IS HATED AND FEARED BY MOST OF HIS PEOPLE.
THE WORLD IS TROUBLED TOO. ARMIES FROM OTHER NATIONS, MOSTLY AMERICA AND BRITAIN, ARE PLANNING TO INVADE IRAQ TO REMOVE SADDAM FROM POWER.
AMID GROWING FEARS OF WAR, DAILY LIFE OF THE IRAQI PEOPLE GOES ON....

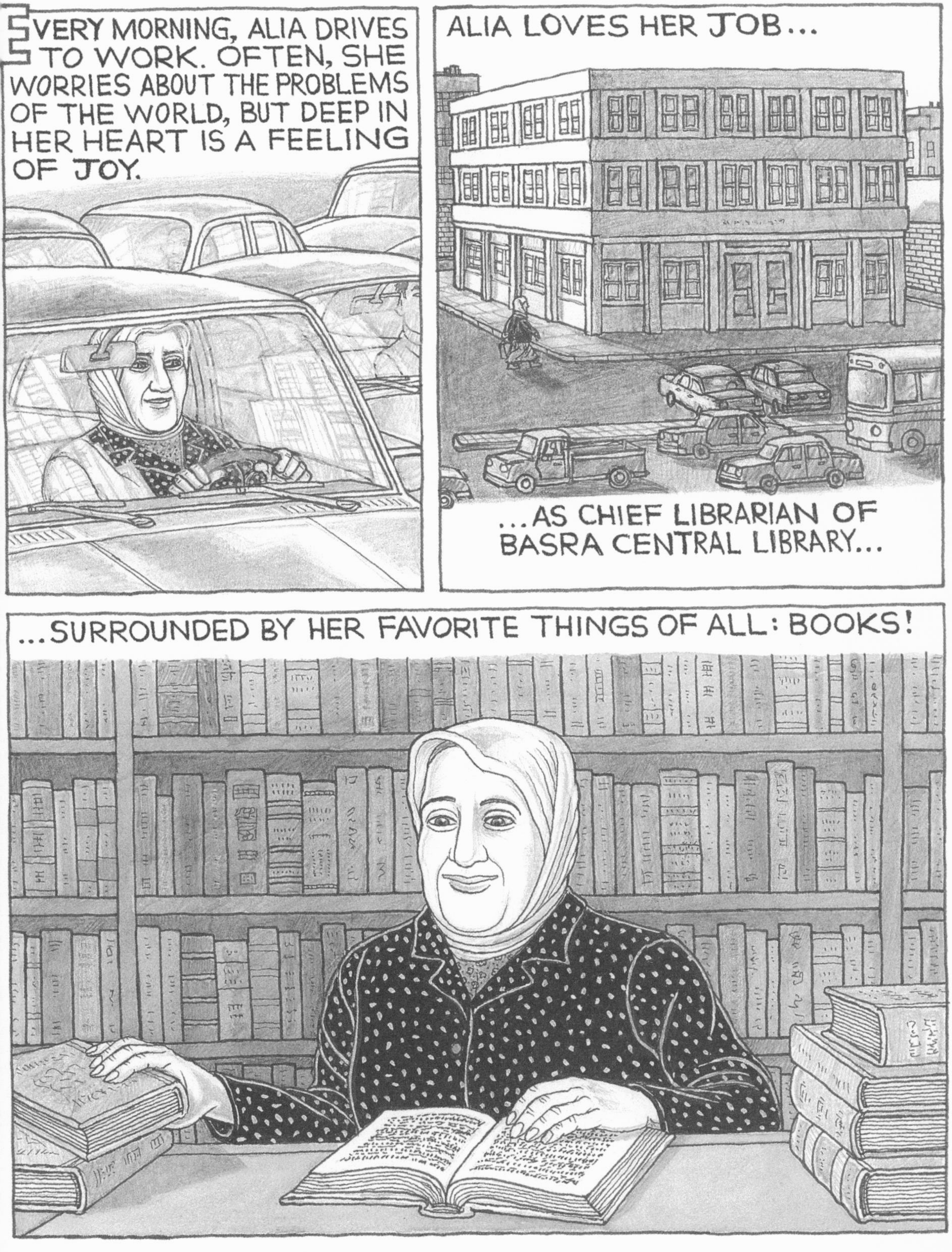
EVERY MORNING, ALIA DRIVES TO WORK. OFTEN, SHE WORRIES ABOUT THE PROBLEMS OF THE WORLD, BUT DEEP IN HER HEART IS A FEELING OF JOY.
ALIA LOVES HER JOB...
...AS CHIEF LIBRARIAN OF BASRA CENTRAL LIBRARY...
...SURROUNDED BY HER FAVORITE THINGS OF ALL: BOOKS!

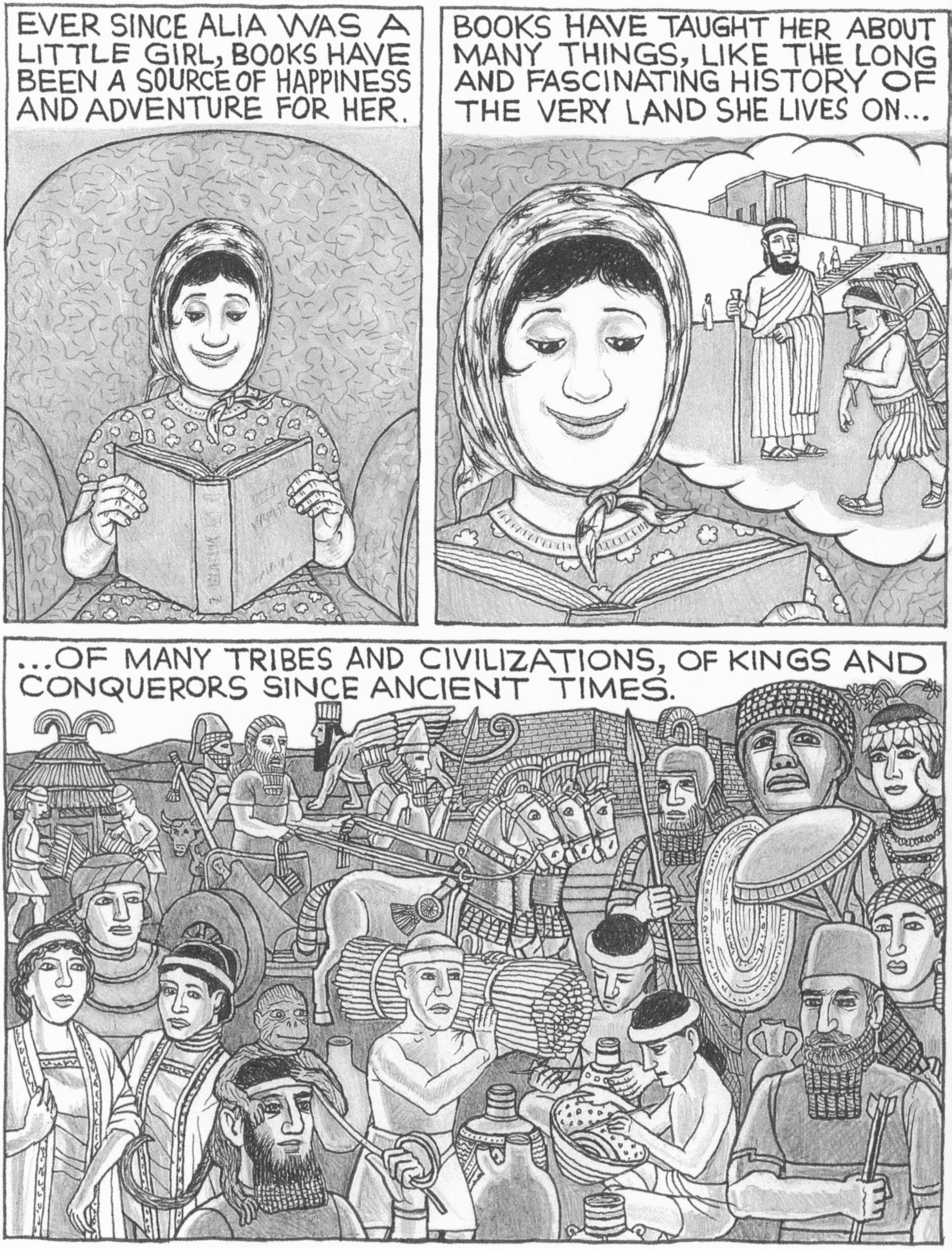
EVER SINCE ALIA WAS A LITTLE GIRL, BOOKS HAVE BEEN A SOURCE OF HAPPINESS AND ADVENTURE FOR HER.
BOOKS HAVE TAUGHT HER ABOUT MANY THINGS, LIKE THE LONG AND FASCINATING HISTORY OF THE VERY LAND SHE LIVES ON...
...OF MANY TRIBES AND CIVILIZATIONS, OF KINGS AND CONQUERORS SINCE ANCIENT TIMES.

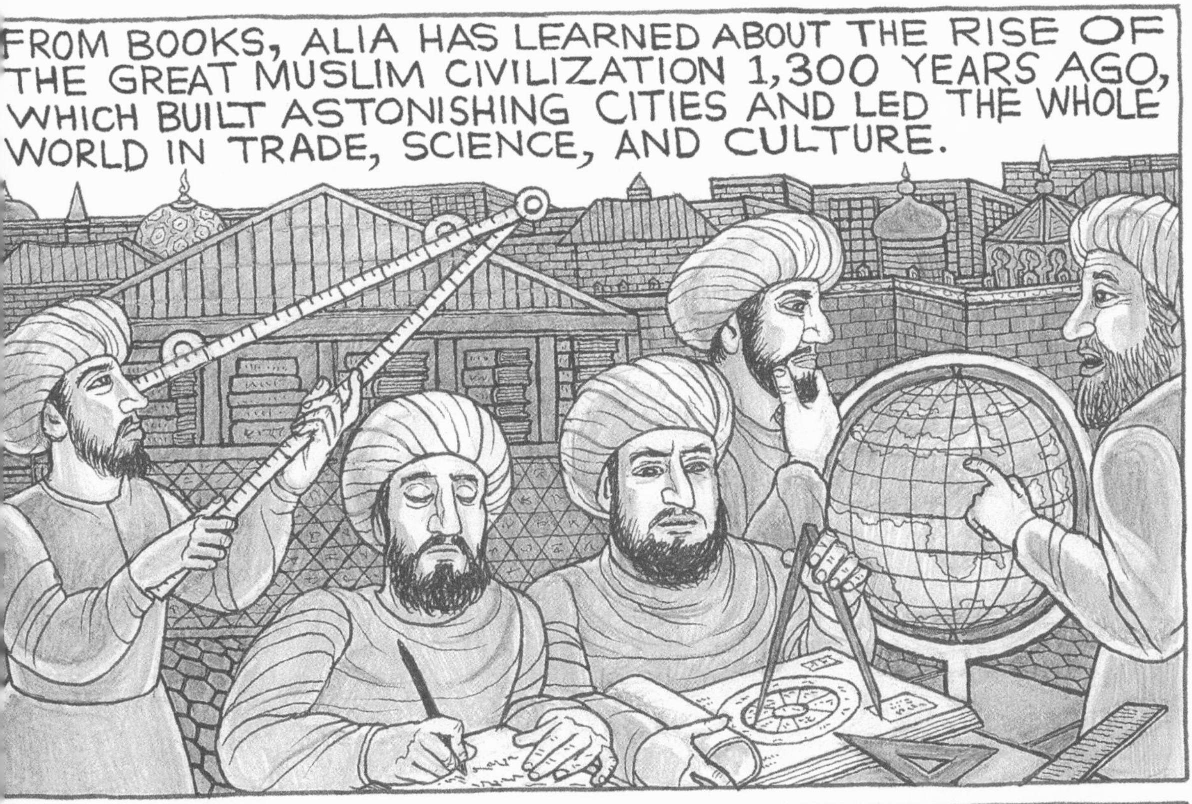
FROM BOOKS, ALIA HAS LEARNED ABOUT THE RISE OF THE GREAT MUSLIM CIVILIZATION 1,300 YEARS AGO, WHICH BUILT ASTONISHING CITIES AND LED THE WHOLE WORLD IN TRADE, SCIENCE, AND CULTURE.

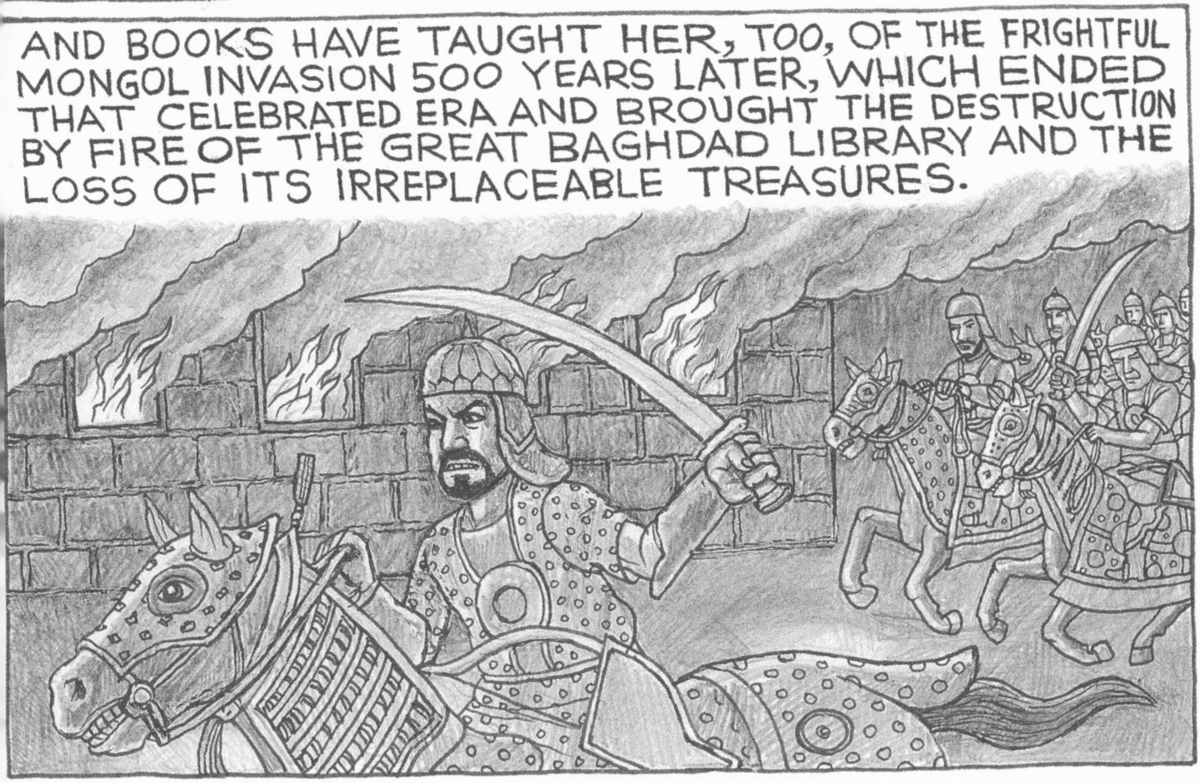
AND BOOKS HAVE TAUGHT HER, TOO, OF THE FRIGHTFUL MONGOL INVASION 500 YEARS LATER, WHICH ENDED THAT CELEBRATED ERA AND BROUGHT THE DESTRUCTION BY FIRE OF THE GREAT BAGHDAD LIBRARY AND THE LOSS OF ITS IRREPLACEABLE TREASURES.

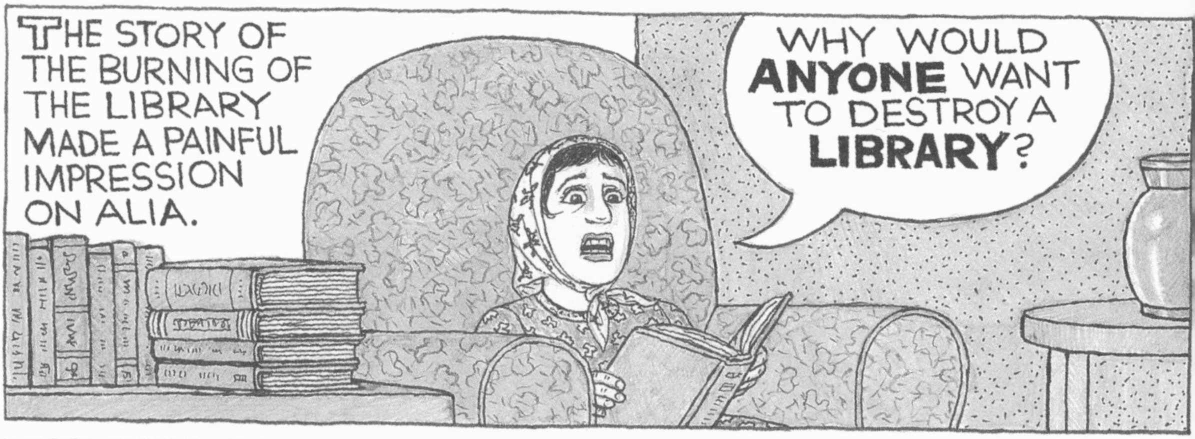
THE STORY OF THE BURNING OF THE LIBRARY MADE A PAINFUL IMPRESSION ON ALIA.
WHY WOULD ANYONE WANT TO DESTROY A LIBRARY?

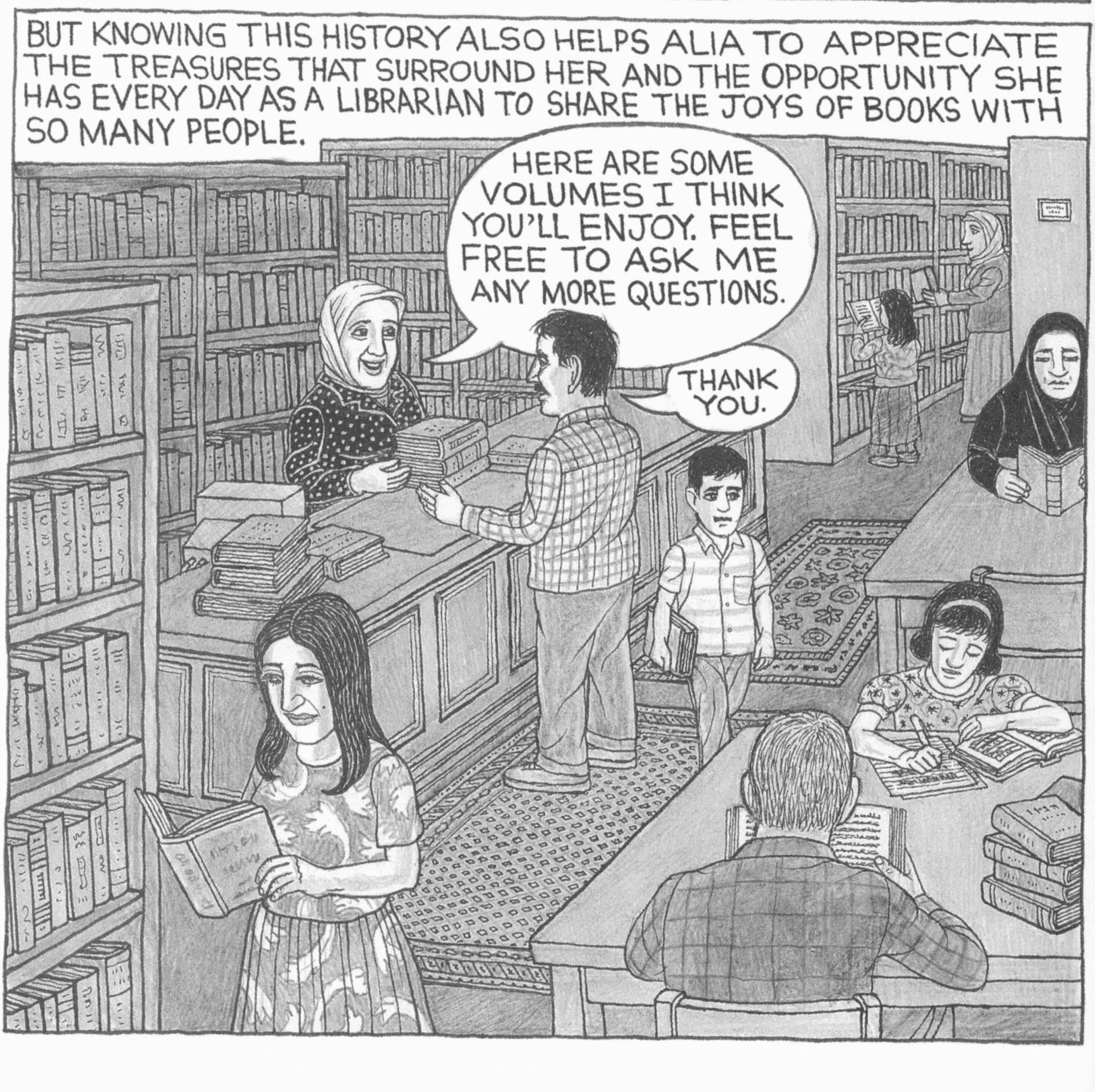
BUT KNOWING THIS HISTORY ALSO HELPS ALIA TO APPRECIATE THE TREASURES THAT SURROUND HER AND THE OPPORTUNITY SHE HAS EVERY DAY AS A LIBRARIAN TO SHARE THE JOYS OF BOOKS WITH SO MANY PEOPLE.
HERE ARE SOME VOLUMES I THINK YOU'LL ENJOY. FEEL FREE TO ASK ME ANY MORE QUESTIONS.
THANK YOU.

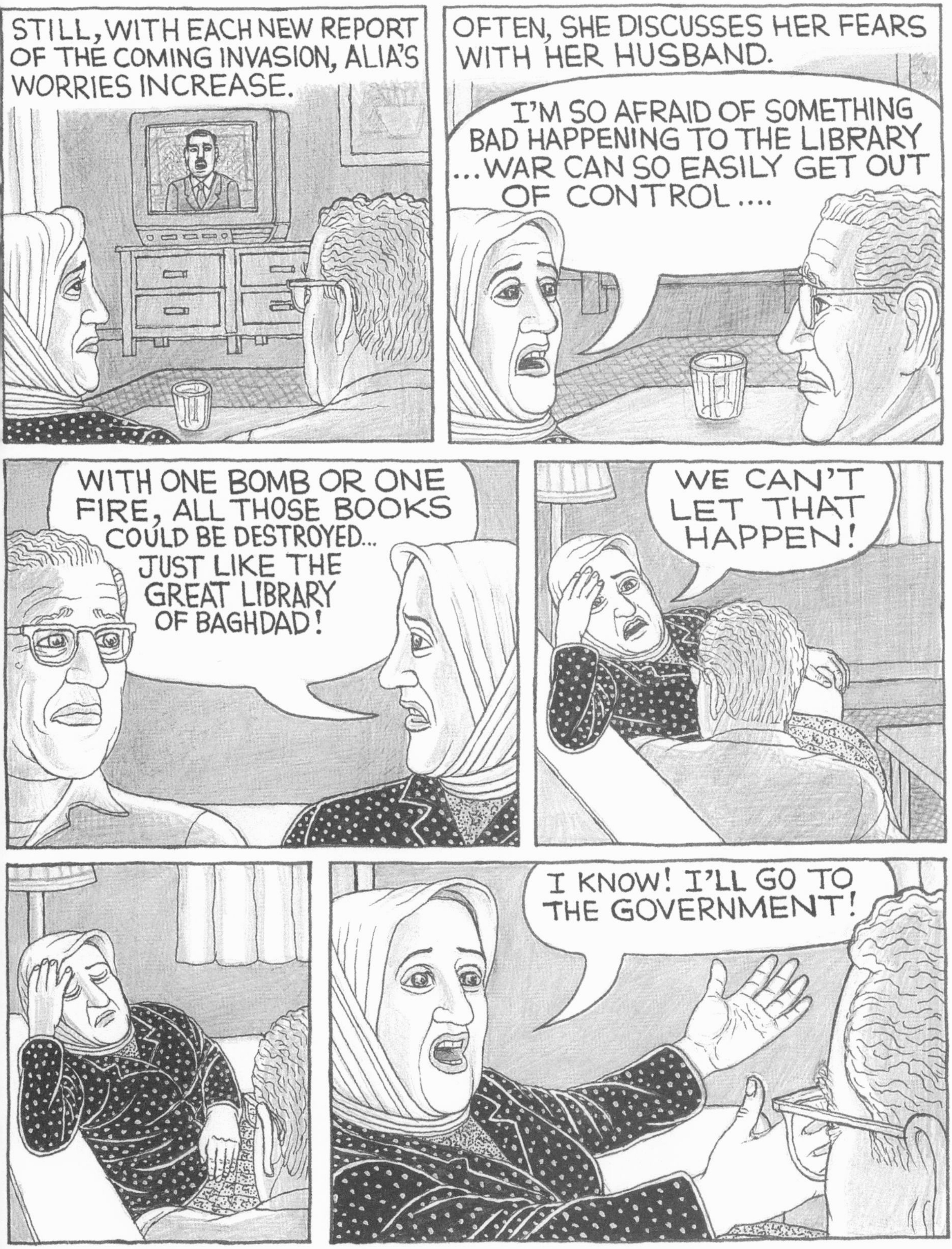
STILL, WITH EACH NEW REPORT OF THE COMING INVASION, ALIA'S WORRIES INCREASE.
OFTEN, SHE DISCUSSES HER FEARS WITH HER HUSBAND.
I'M SO AFRAID OF SOMETHING BAD HAPPENING TO THE LIBRARY ...WAR CAN SO EASILY GET OUT OF CONTROL....
WITH ONE BOMB OR ONE FIRE, ALL THOSE BOOKS COULD BE DESTROYED... JUST LIKE THE GREAT LIBRARY OF BAGHDAD!
WE CAN'T LET THAT HAPPEN!
I KNOW! I'LL GO TO THE GOVERNMENT!

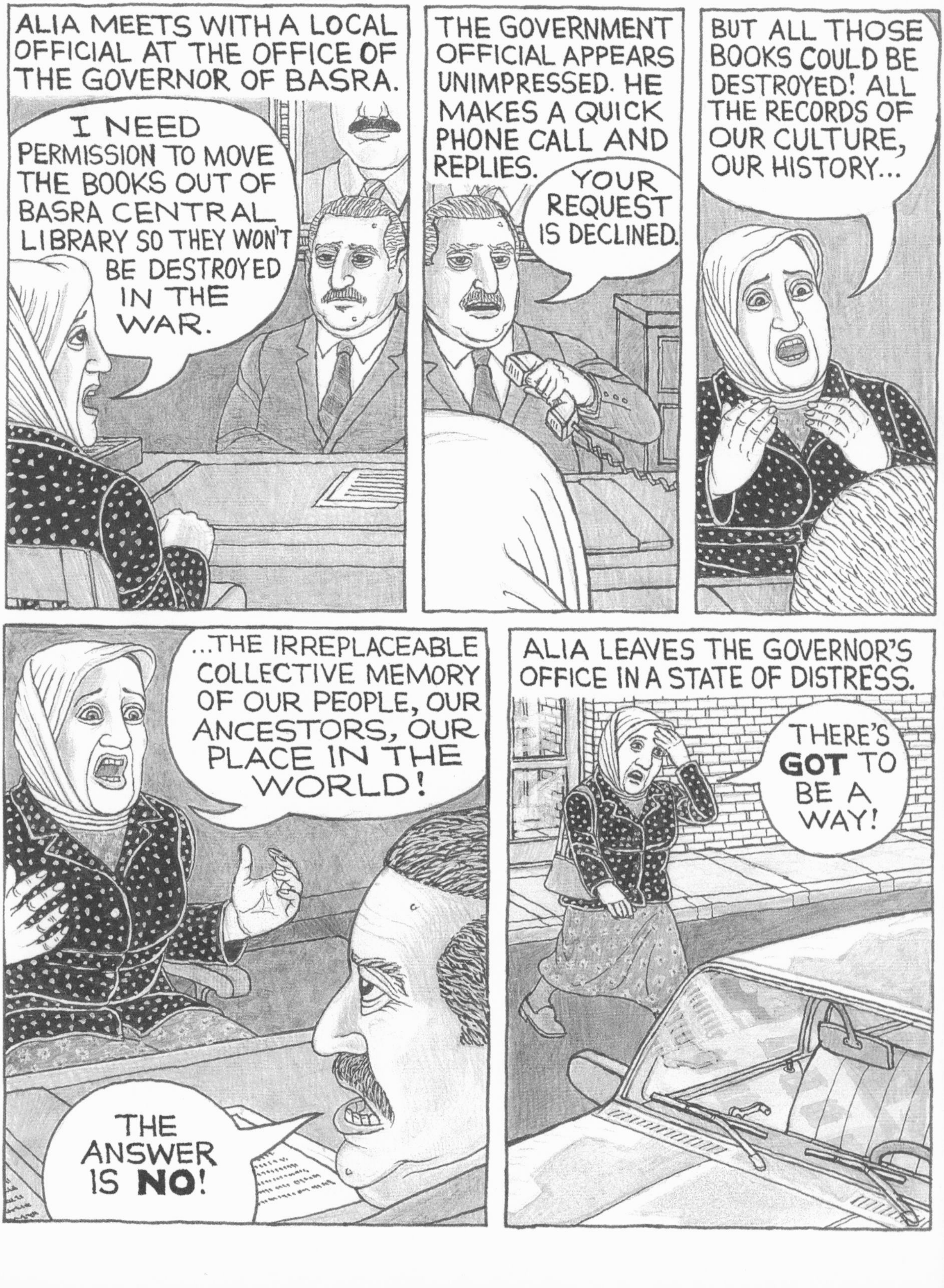
ALIA MEETS WITH A LOCAL OFFICIAL AT THE OFFICE OF THE GOVERNOR OF BASRA.
I NEED PERMISSION TO MOVE THE BOOKS OUT OF BASRA CENTRAL LIBRARY SO THEY WON'T BE DESTROYED IN THE WAR.
THE GOVERNMENT OFFICIAL APPEARS UNIMPRESSED. HE MAKES A QUICK PHONE CALL AND REPLIES.
YOUR REQUEST IS DECLINED.
BUT ALL THOSE BOOKS COULD BE DESTROYED! ALL THE RECORDS OF OUR CULTURE, OUR HISTORY...
...THE IRREPLACEABLE COLLECTIVE MEMORY OF OUR PEOPLE, OUR ANCESTORS, OUR PLACE IN THE WORLD!
THE ANSWER IS **NO**!
ALIA LEAVES THE GOVERNOR'S OFFICE IN A STATE OF DISTRESS.
THERE'S **GOT** TO BE A WAY!

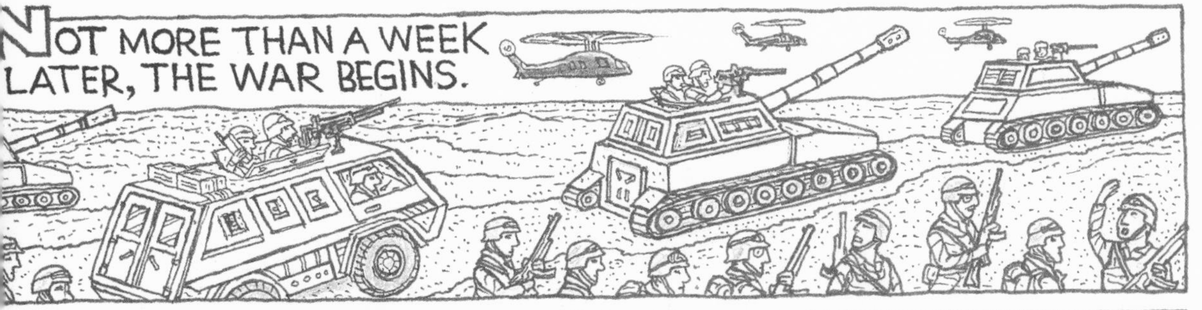
NOT MORE THAN A WEEK LATER, THE WAR BEGINS.

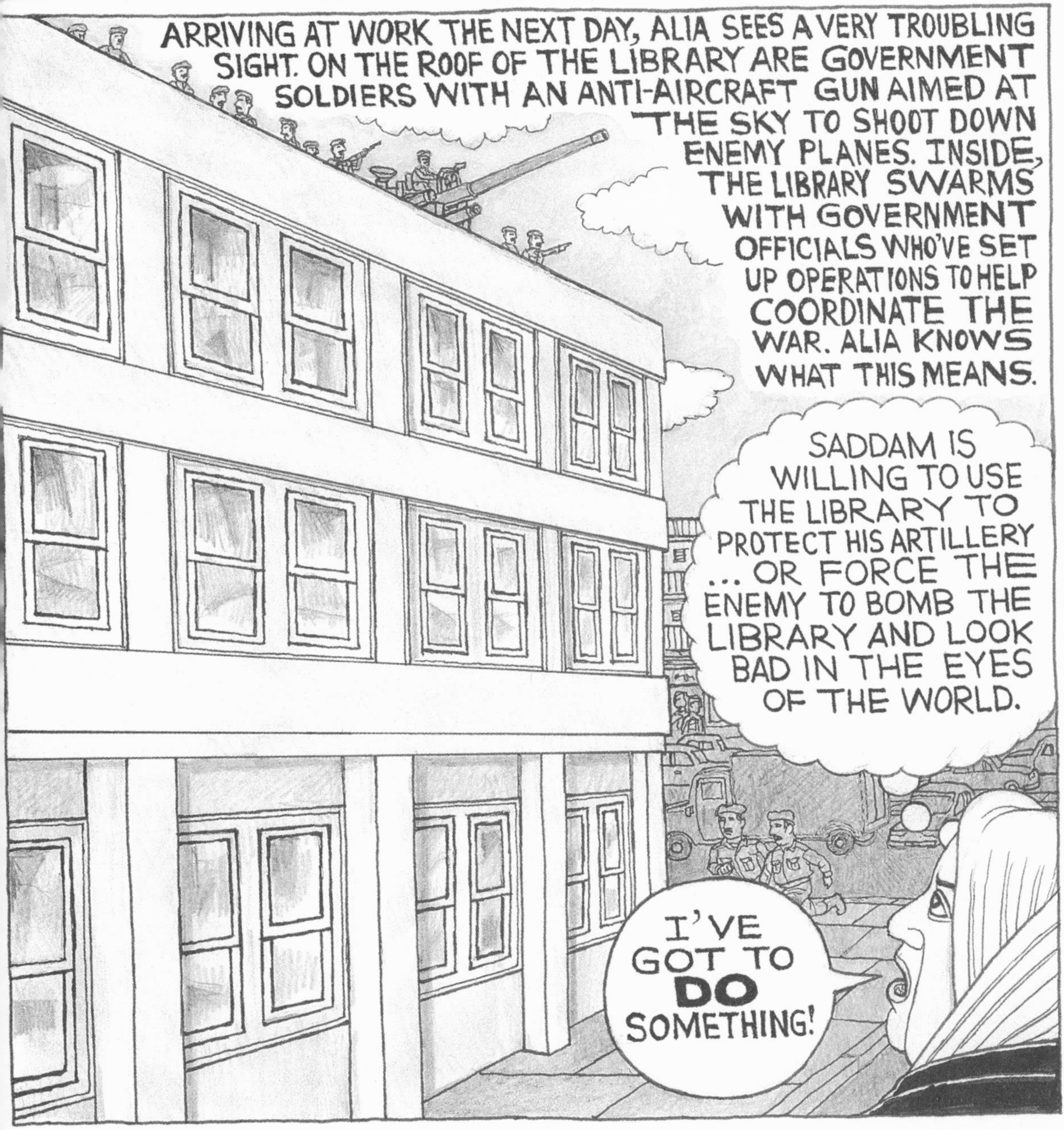
ARRIVING AT WORK THE NEXT DAY, ALIA SEES A VERY TROUBLING SIGHT. ON THE ROOF OF THE LIBRARY ARE GOVERNMENT SOLDIERS WITH AN ANTI-AIRCRAFT GUN AIMED AT THE SKY TO SHOOT DOWN ENEMY PLANES. INSIDE, THE LIBRARY SWARMS WITH GOVERNMENT OFFICIALS WHO'VE SET UP OPERATIONS TO HELP COORDINATE THE WAR. ALIA KNOWS WHAT THIS MEANS.
SADDAM IS WILLING TO USE THE LIBRARY TO PROTECT HIS ARTILLERY ... OR FORCE THE ENEMY TO BOMB THE LIBRARY AND LOOK BAD IN THE EYES OF THE WORLD.
I'VE GOT TO **DO** SOMETHING!

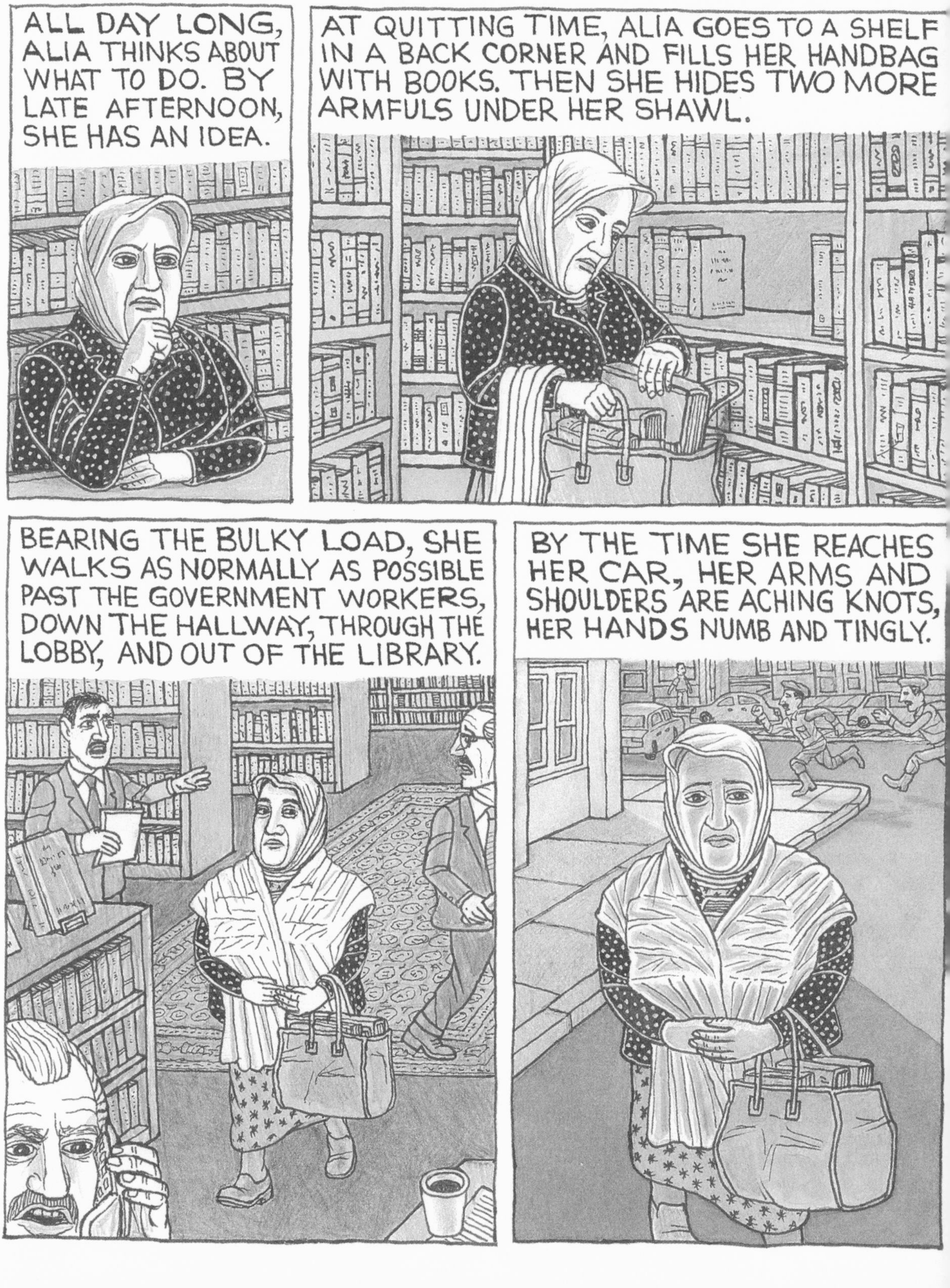
ALL DAY LONG, ALIA THINKS ABOUT WHAT TO DO. BY LATE AFTERNOON, SHE HAS AN IDEA.
AT QUITTING TIME, ALIA GOES TO A SHELF IN A BACK CORNER AND FILLS HER HANDBAG WITH BOOKS. THEN SHE HIDES TWO MORE ARMFULS UNDER HER SHAWL.
BEARING THE BULKY LOAD, SHE WALKS AS NORMALLY AS POSSIBLE PAST THE GOVERNMENT WORKERS, DOWN THE HALLWAY, THROUGH THE LOBBY, AND OUT OF THE LIBRARY.
BY THE TIME SHE REACHES HER CAR, HER ARMS AND SHOULDERS ARE ACHING KNOTS, HER HANDS NUMB AND TINGLY.

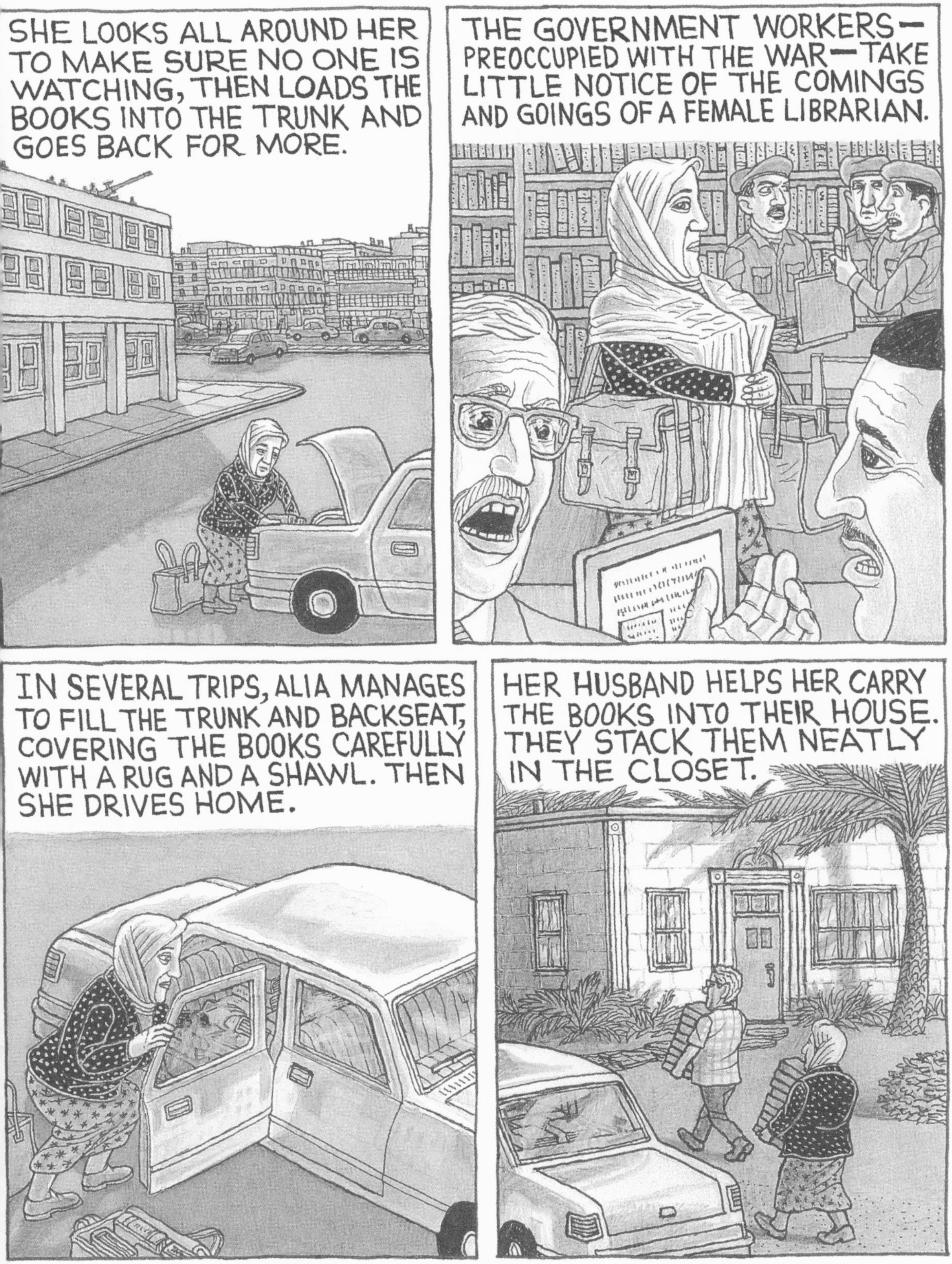
SHE LOOKS ALL AROUND HER TO MAKE SURE NO ONE IS WATCHING, THEN LOADS THE BOOKS INTO THE TRUNK AND GOES BACK FOR MORE.
THE GOVERNMENT WORKERS— PREOCCUPIED WITH THE WAR—TAKE LITTLE NOTICE OF THE COMINGS AND GOINGS OF A FEMALE LIBRARIAN.
IN SEVERAL TRIPS, ALIA MANAGES TO FILL THE TRUNK AND BACKSEAT, COVERING THE BOOKS CAREFULLY WITH A RUG AND A SHAWL. THEN SHE DRIVES HOME.
HER HUSBAND HELPS HER CARRY THE BOOKS INTO THEIR HOUSE. THEY STACK THEM NEATLY IN THE CLOSET.

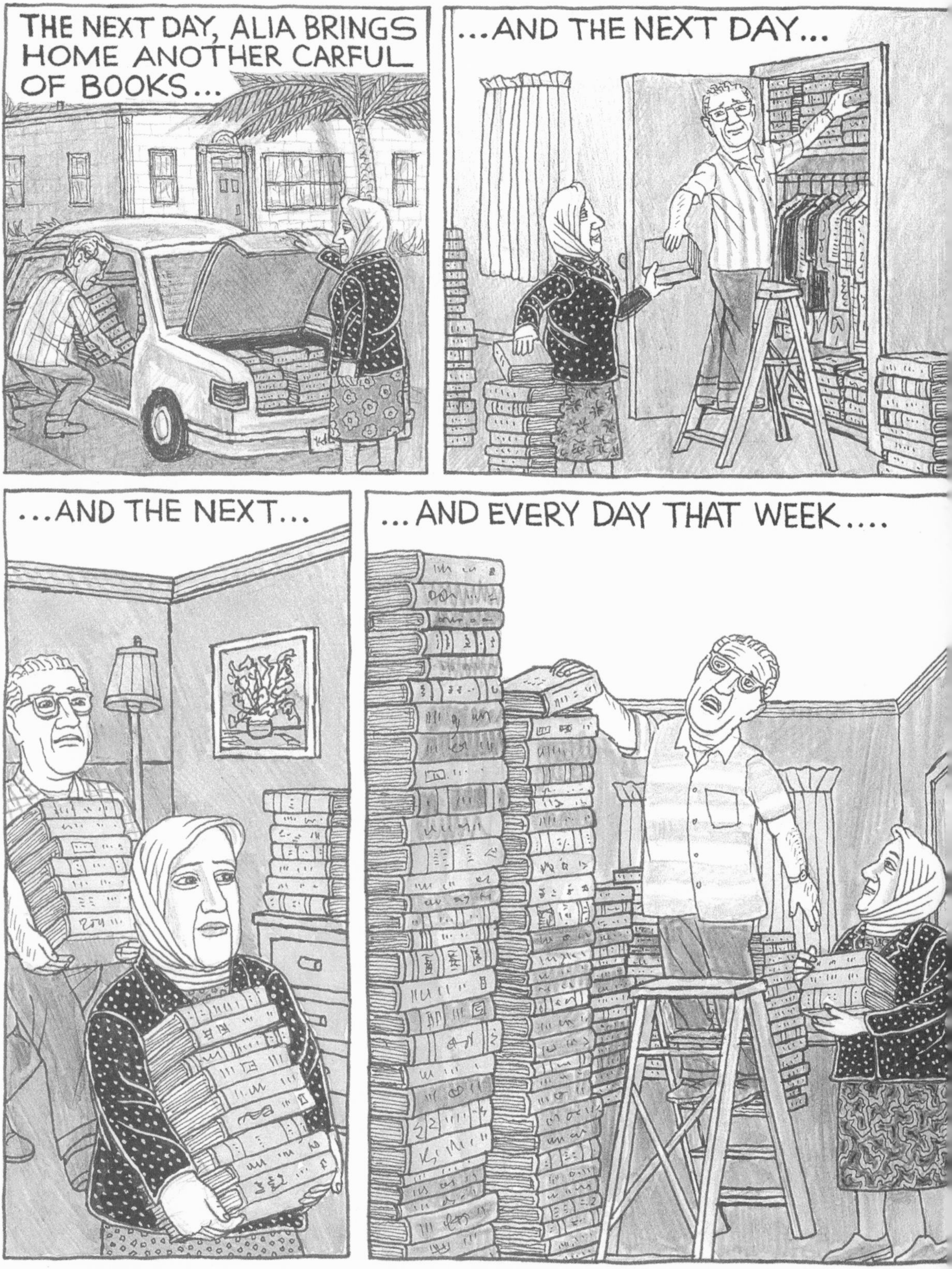
THE NEXT DAY, ALIA BRINGS HOME ANOTHER CARFUL OF BOOKS...
...AND THE NEXT DAY...
...AND THE NEXT...
...AND EVERY DAY THAT WEEK....

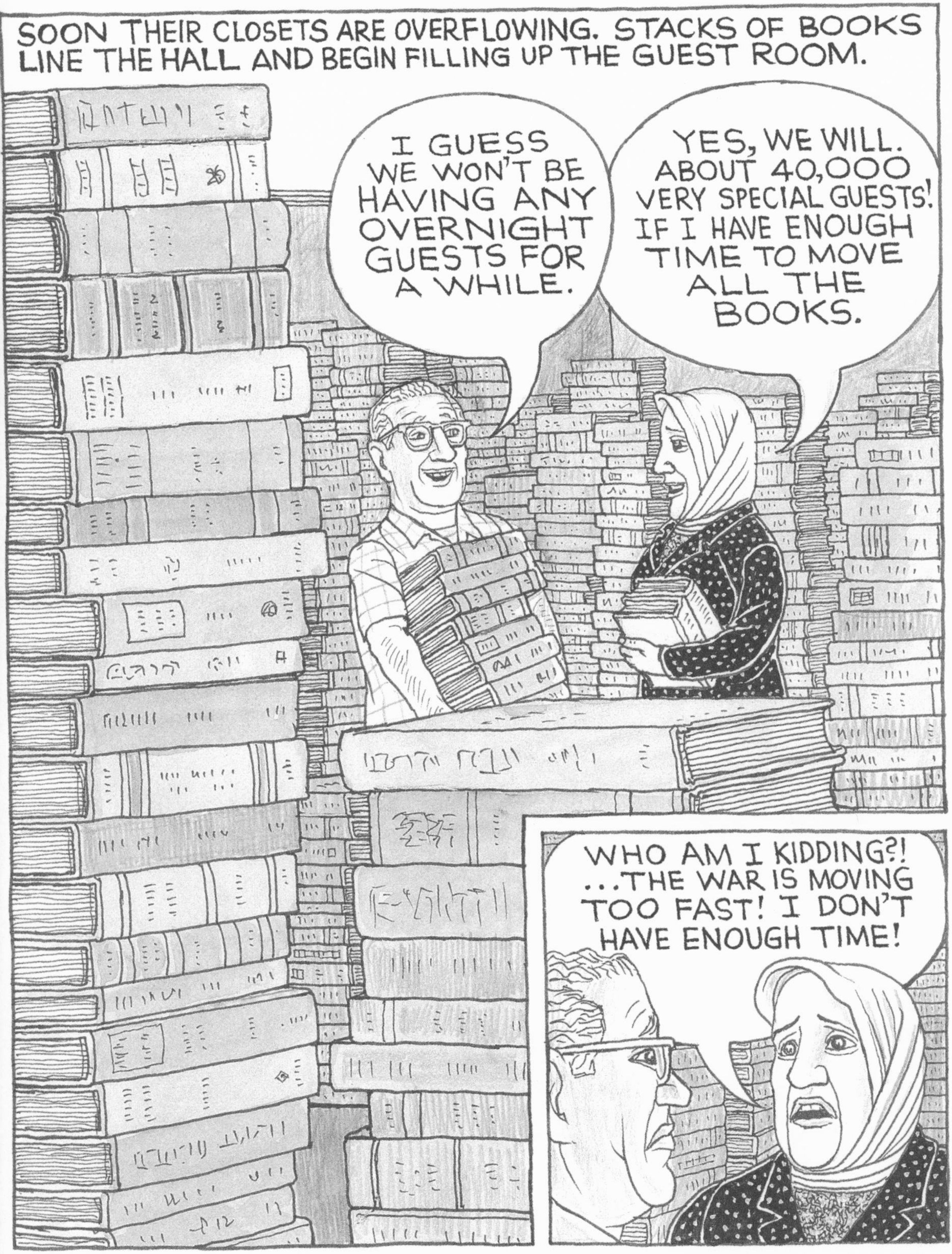
SOON THEIR CLOSETS ARE OVERFLOWING. STACKS OF BOOKS LINE THE HALL AND BEGIN FILLING UP THE GUEST ROOM.
I GUESS WE WON'T BE HAVING ANY OVERNIGHT GUESTS FOR A WHILE.
YES, WE WILL. ABOUT 40,000 VERY SPECIAL GUESTS! IF I HAVE ENOUGH TIME TO MOVE ALL THE BOOKS.
WHO AM I KIDDING?! ...THE WAR IS MOVING TOO FAST! I DON'T HAVE ENOUGH TIME!

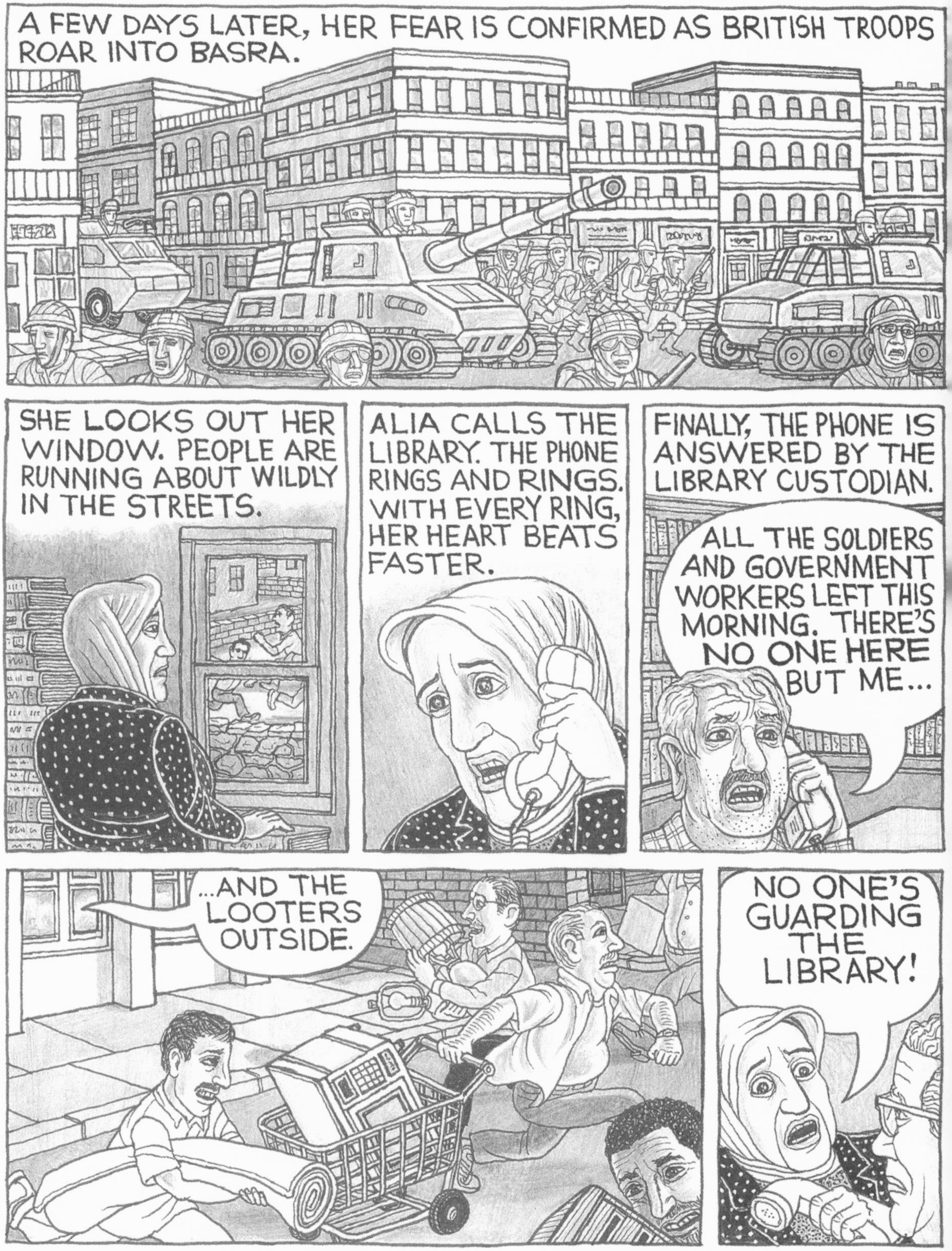
A FEW DAYS LATER, HER FEAR IS CONFIRMED AS BRITISH TROOPS ROAR INTO BASRA.
SHE LOOKS OUT HER WINDOW. PEOPLE ARE RUNNING ABOUT WILDLY IN THE STREETS.
ALIA CALLS THE LIBRARY. THE PHONE RINGS AND RINGS. WITH EVERY RING, HER HEART BEATS FASTER.
FINALLY, THE PHONE IS ANSWERED BY THE LIBRARY CUSTODIAN.
ALL THE SOLDIERS AND GOVERNMENT WORKERS LEFT THIS MORNING. THERE'S NO ONE HERE BUT ME...
...AND THE LOOTERS OUTSIDE.
NO ONE'S GUARDING THE LIBRARY!

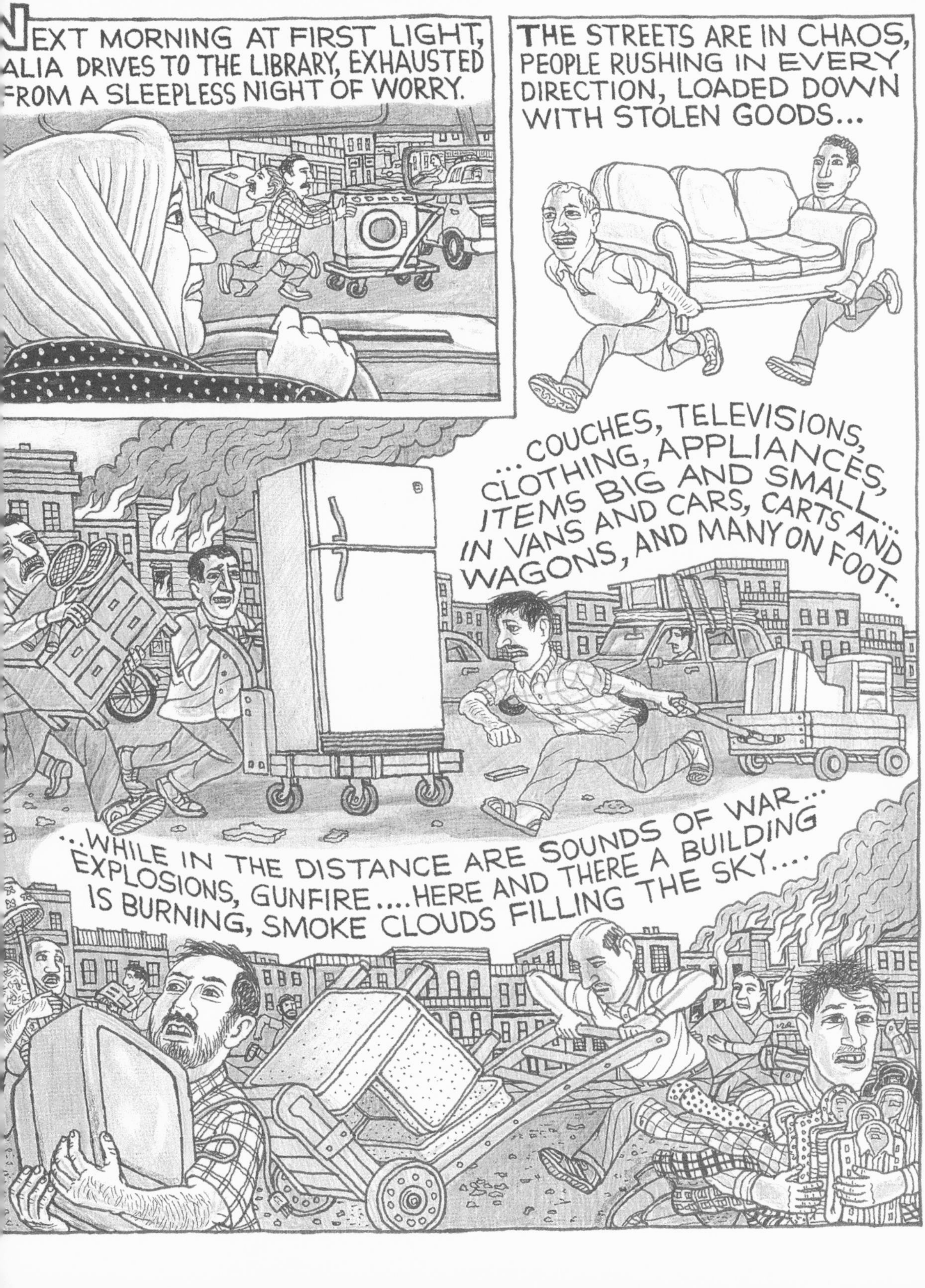
NEXT MORNING AT FIRST LIGHT, ALIA DRIVES TO THE LIBRARY, EXHAUSTED FROM A SLEEPLESS NIGHT OF WORRY.
THE STREETS ARE IN CHAOS, PEOPLE RUSHING IN EVERY DIRECTION, LOADED DOWN WITH STOLEN GOODS...
...COUCHES, TELEVISIONS, CLOTHING, APPLIANCES, ITEMS BIG AND SMALL... IN VANS AND CARS, CARTS AND WAGONS, AND MANY ON FOOT...
...WHILE IN THE DISTANCE ARE SOUNDS OF WAR... EXPLOSIONS, GUNFIRE.... HERE AND THERE A BUILDING IS BURNING, SMOKE CLOUDS FILLING THE SKY....

ARRIVING AT LAST AT THE LIBRARY, ALIA HURRIES INSIDE. THE LOOTERS HAVE BEEN HERE! GONE ARE THE CARPETS AND TABLES, LIGHTS AND FIXTURES, AND WHO KNOWS WHAT ELSE?!

THEY EVEN TOOK THE PENCIL SHARPENERS AND THE VACUUM CLEANER AND THE COFFEEMAKER . . . .

THE ONLY THING THEY DIDN'T TAKE IS...

...THE **BOOKS!**

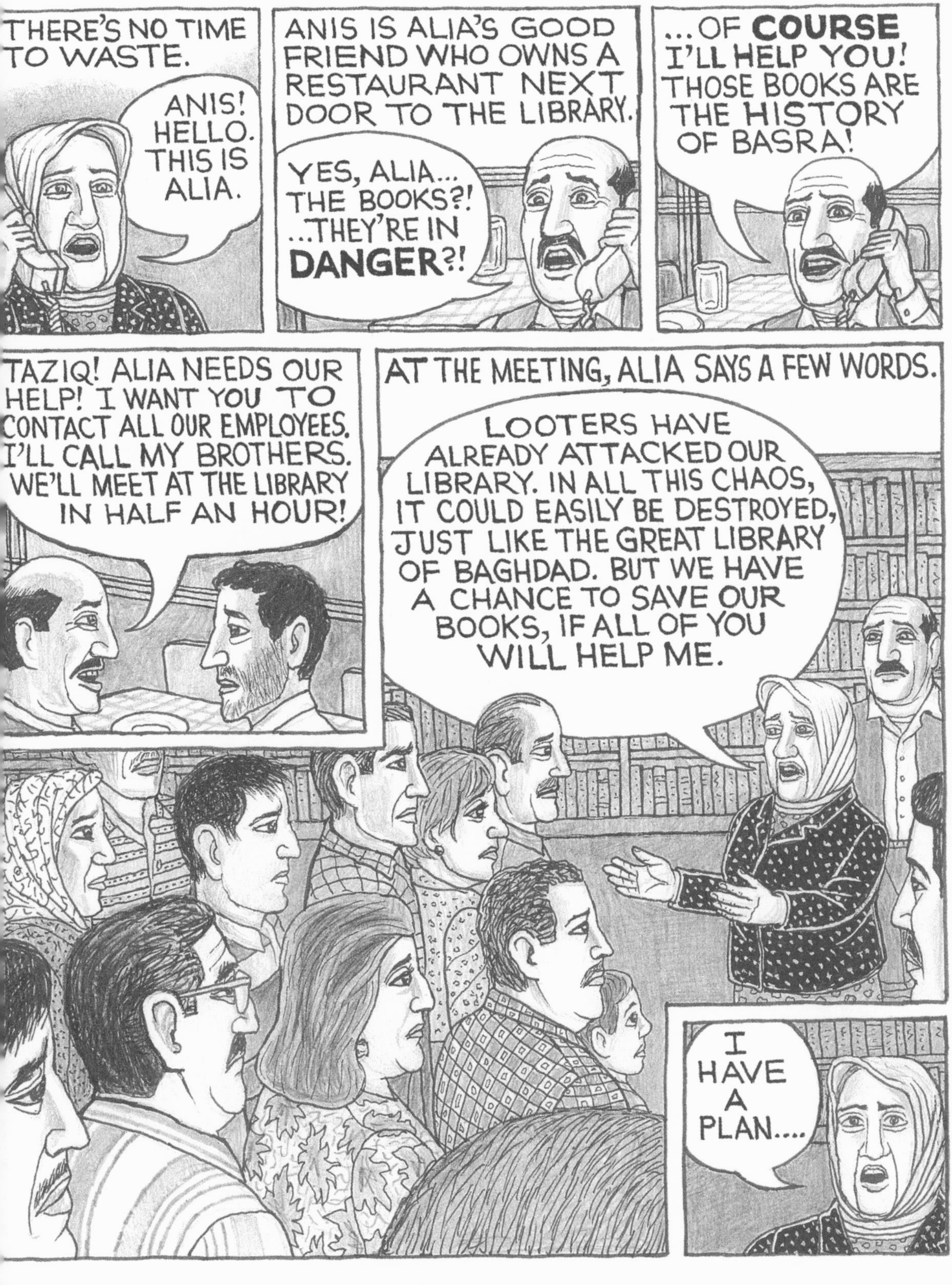
THERE'S NO TIME TO WASTE.
ANIS! HELLO. THIS IS ALIA.
ANIS IS ALIA'S GOOD FRIEND WHO OWNS A RESTAURANT NEXT DOOR TO THE LIBRARY.
YES, ALIA... THE BOOKS?! ...THEY'RE IN DANGER?!
...OF COURSE I'LL HELP YOU! THOSE BOOKS ARE THE HISTORY OF BASRA!
TAZIQ! ALIA NEEDS OUR HELP! I WANT YOU TO CONTACT ALL OUR EMPLOYEES. I'LL CALL MY BROTHERS. WE'LL MEET AT THE LIBRARY IN HALF AN HOUR!
AT THE MEETING, ALIA SAYS A FEW WORDS.
LOOTERS HAVE ALREADY ATTACKED OUR LIBRARY. IN ALL THIS CHAOS, IT COULD EASILY BE DESTROYED, JUST LIKE THE GREAT LIBRARY OF BAGHDAD. BUT WE HAVE A CHANCE TO SAVE OUR BOOKS, IF ALL OF YOU WILL HELP ME.
I HAVE A PLAN....

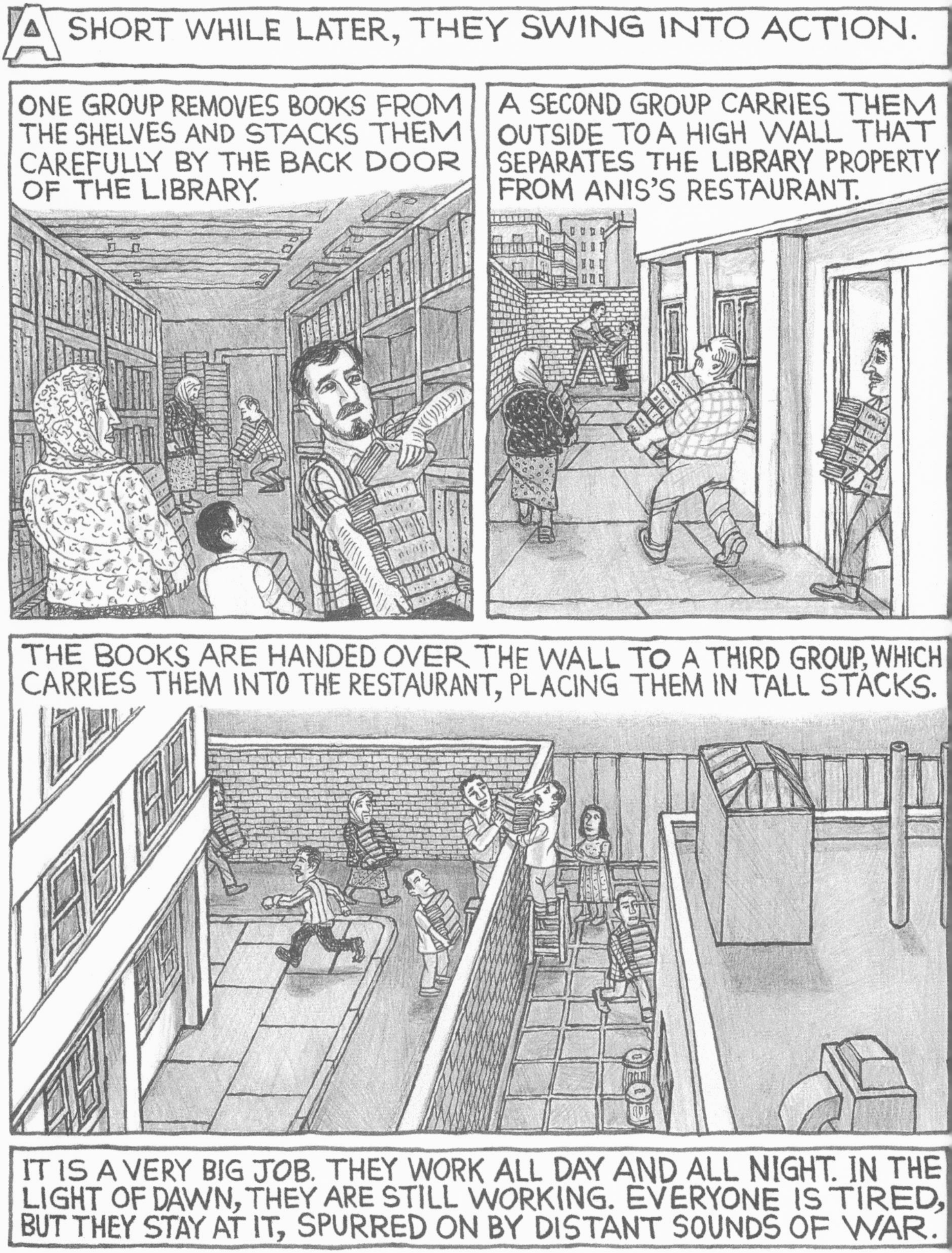
A SHORT WHILE LATER, THEY SWING INTO ACTION.
ONE GROUP REMOVES BOOKS FROM THE SHELVES AND STACKS THEM CAREFULLY BY THE BACK DOOR OF THE LIBRARY.
A SECOND GROUP CARRIES THEM OUTSIDE TO A HIGH WALL THAT SEPARATES THE LIBRARY PROPERTY FROM ANIS'S RESTAURANT.
THE BOOKS ARE HANDED OVER THE WALL TO A THIRD GROUP, WHICH CARRIES THEM INTO THE RESTAURANT, PLACING THEM IN TALL STACKS.
IT IS A VERY BIG JOB. THEY WORK ALL DAY AND ALL NIGHT. IN THE LIGHT OF DAWN, THEY ARE STILL WORKING. EVERYONE IS TIRED, BUT THEY STAY AT IT, SPURRED ON BY DISTANT SOUNDS OF WAR.

AS THE DAY PROGRESSES, MORE AND MORE LOCAL PEOPLE JOIN IN... SHOPKEEPERS, NEIGHBORS, PASSERSBY... SOME OF THEM EDUCATED PEOPLE WHO READ A LOT AND OTHERS WHO READ LESS OR CAN'T READ AT ALL.

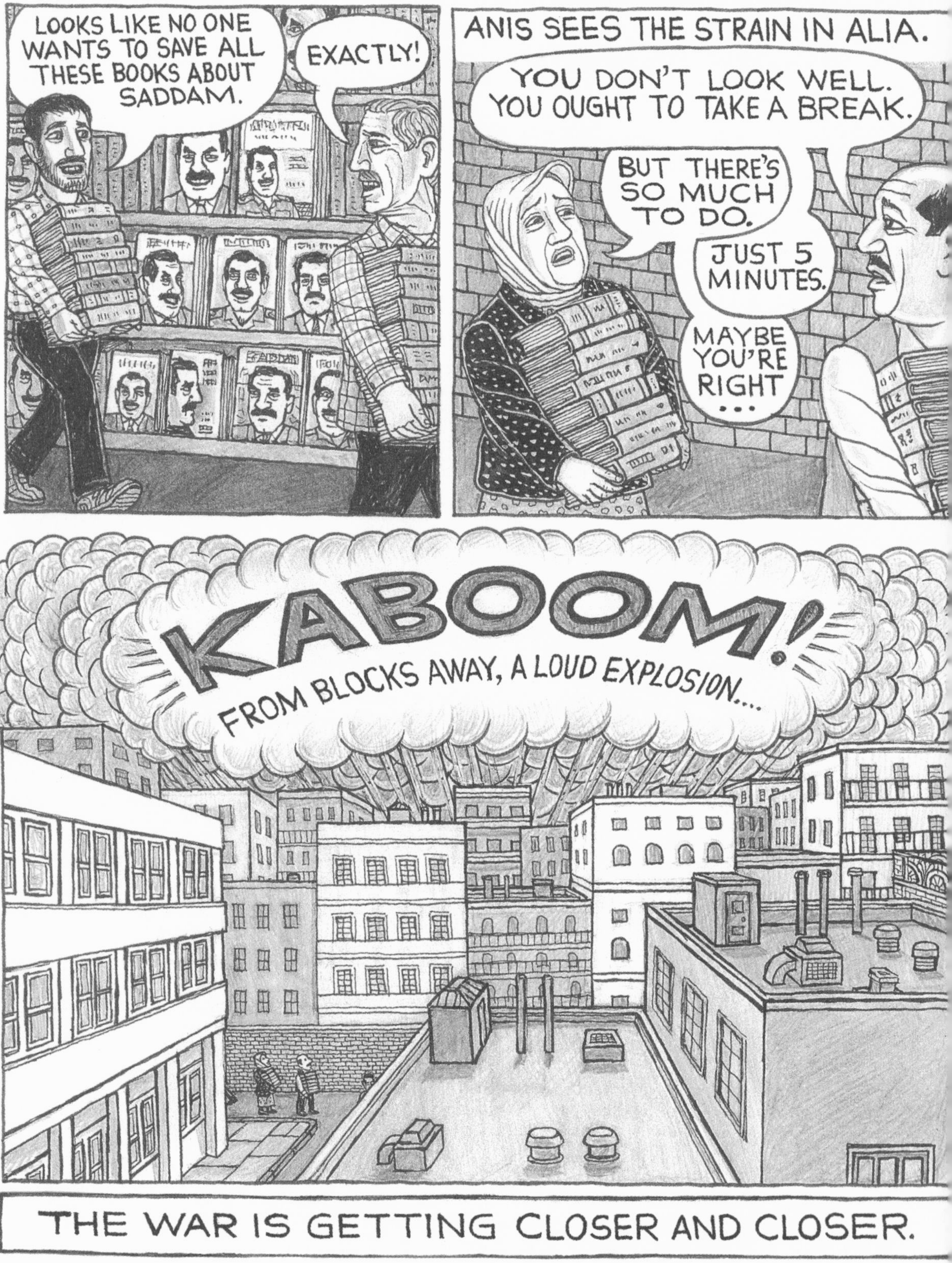
LOOKS LIKE NO ONE WANTS TO SAVE ALL THESE BOOKS ABOUT SADDAM.
EXACTLY!
ANIS SEES THE STRAIN IN ALIA.
YOU DON'T LOOK WELL. YOU OUGHT TO TAKE A BREAK.
BUT THERE'S SO MUCH TO DO.
JUST 5 MINUTES.
MAYBE YOU'RE RIGHT...
KABOOM!
FROM BLOCKS AWAY, A LOUD EXPLOSION....
THE WAR IS GETTING CLOSER AND CLOSER.

CLOUDS OF SMOKE FROM THE EXPLOSION FILL THE AIR.

I'LL SLEEP TONIGHT. RIGHT NOW, EVERY MINUTE COUNTS.

THEY WORK TILL CLOSE TO MIDNIGHT, THEN CALL IT A DAY.

GOOD NIGHT, ALIA. SEE YOU IN THE MORNING.

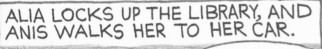

ALIA LOCKS UP THE LIBRARY, AND ANIS WALKS HER TO HER CAR.

I WISH I HAD THE STRENGTH TO WORK ALL NIGHT AGAIN TONIGHT AND EVERY NIGHT TILL ALL THE BOOKS ARE SAFE!

YOU'RE ONLY HUMAN, ALIA. YOU'RE DOING THE BEST YOU CAN.

THREE HOURS LATER, SHE IS SOUND ASLEEP, DREAMING OF BOOKS, WHEN THE PHONE RINGS....

...hello...

NO!!

THE LIBRARY'S ON FIRE! I'VE GOT TO GET THERE RIGHT AWAY!

I'LL DRIVE YOU.

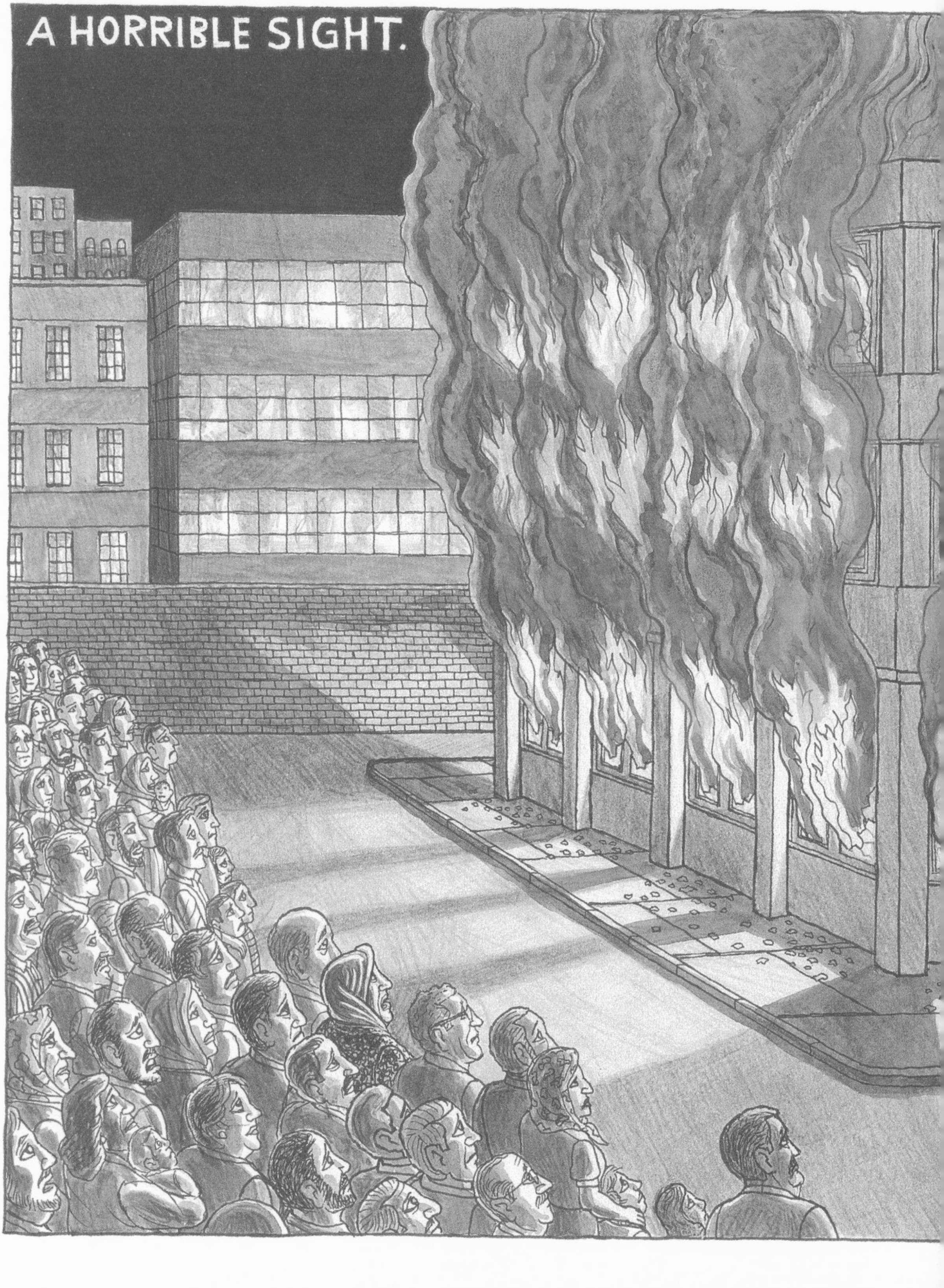
A HORRIBLE SIGHT.

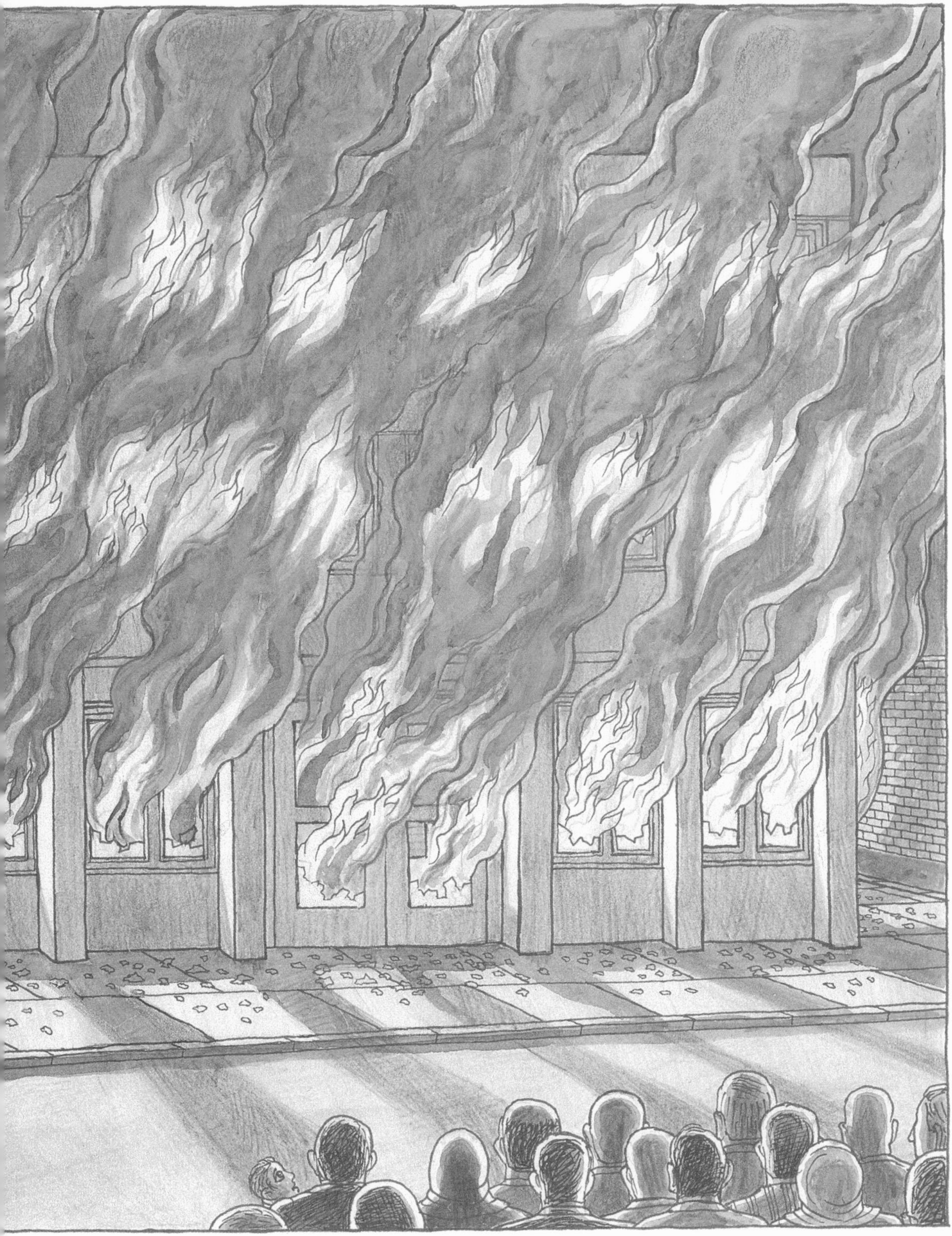

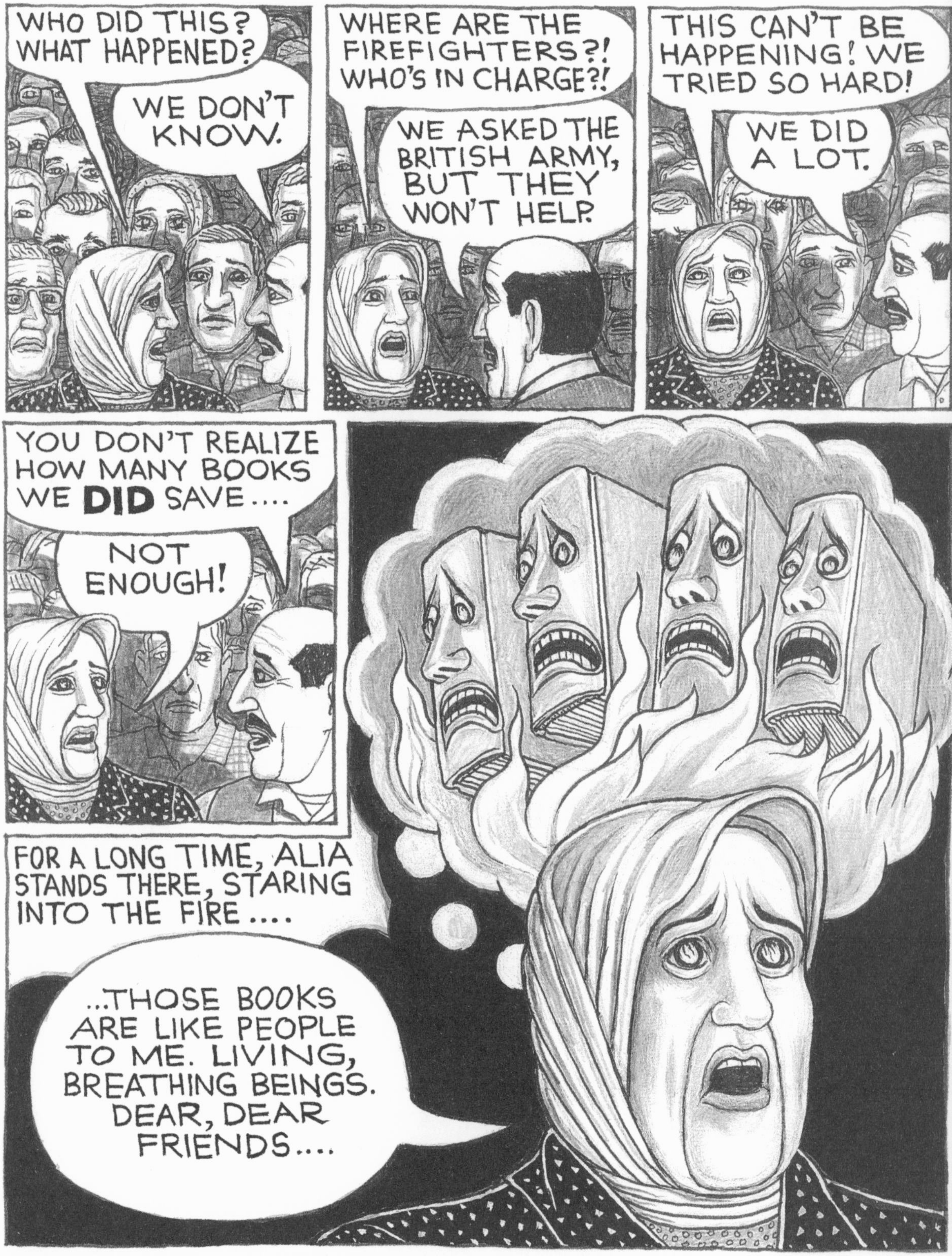
WHO DID THIS? WHAT HAPPENED?
WE DON'T KNOW.
WHERE ARE THE FIREFIGHTERS?! WHO'S IN CHARGE?!
WE ASKED THE BRITISH ARMY, BUT THEY WON'T HELP.
THIS CAN'T BE HAPPENING! WE TRIED SO HARD!
WE DID A LOT.
YOU DON'T REALIZE HOW MANY BOOKS WE **DID** SAVE....
NOT ENOUGH!
FOR A LONG TIME, ALIA STANDS THERE, STARING INTO THE FIRE....
...THOSE BOOKS ARE LIKE PEOPLE TO ME. LIVING, BREATHING BEINGS. DEAR, DEAR FRIENDS....

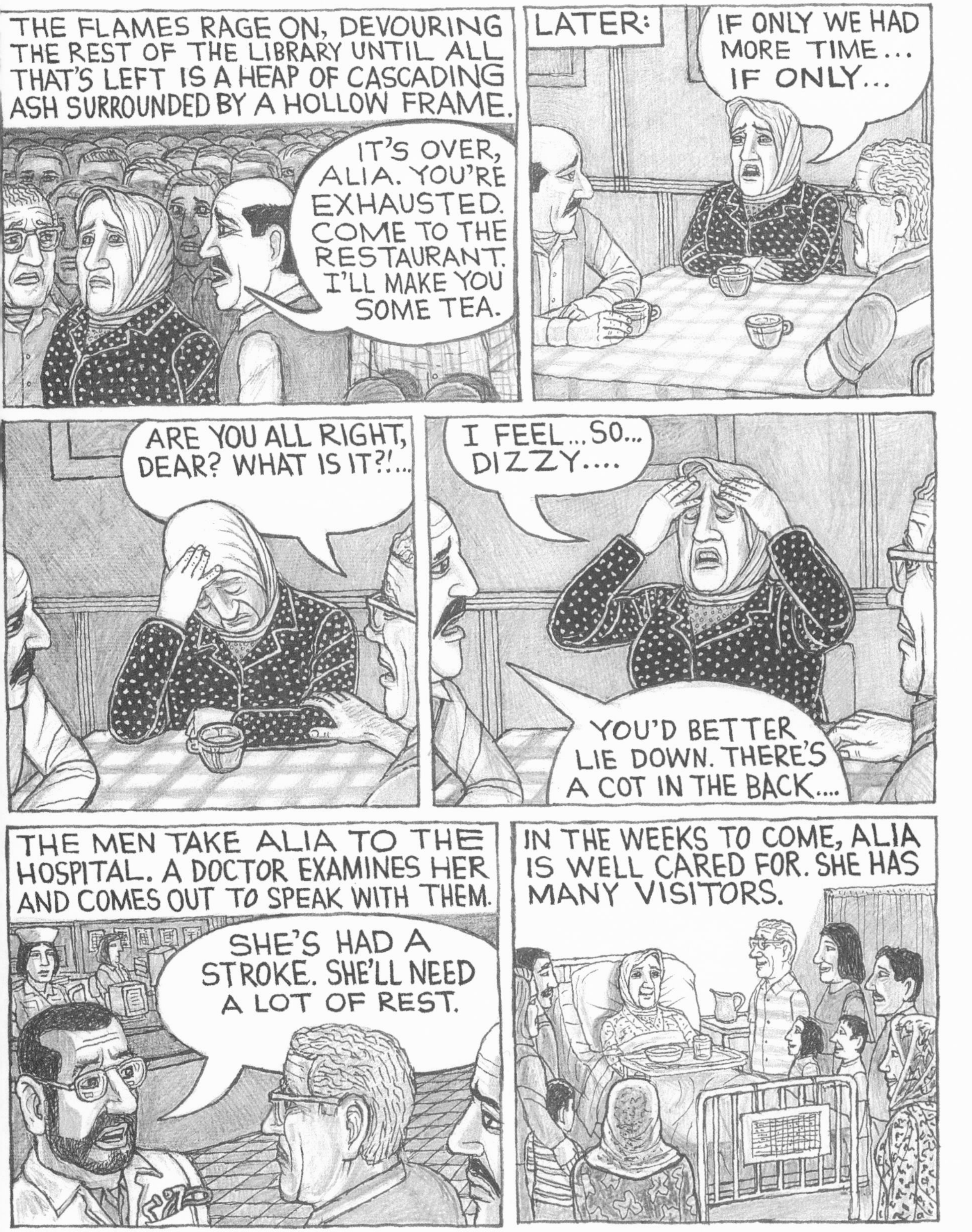
THE FLAMES RAGE ON, DEVOURING THE REST OF THE LIBRARY UNTIL ALL THAT'S LEFT IS A HEAP OF CASCADING ASH SURROUNDED BY A HOLLOW FRAME.
IT'S OVER, ALIA. YOU'RE EXHAUSTED. COME TO THE RESTAURANT. I'LL MAKE YOU SOME TEA.
LATER:
IF ONLY WE HAD MORE TIME... IF ONLY...
ARE YOU ALL RIGHT, DEAR? WHAT IS IT?!...
I FEEL...SO... DIZZY....
YOU'D BETTER LIE DOWN. THERE'S A COT IN THE BACK....
THE MEN TAKE ALIA TO THE HOSPITAL. A DOCTOR EXAMINES HER AND COMES OUT TO SPEAK WITH THEM.
SHE'S HAD A STROKE. SHE'LL NEED A LOT OF REST.
IN THE WEEKS TO COME, ALIA IS WELL CARED FOR. SHE HAS MANY VISITORS.

SHE CONTINUES HER RECOVERY AT HOME. ONE DAY, ANIS COMES TO VISIT.

HOW ARE YOU FEELING?

BETTER. MUCH BETTER.

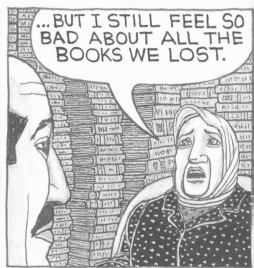

...BUT I STILL FEEL SO BAD ABOUT ALL THE BOOKS WE LOST.

BUT WE **SAVED** A LOT MORE BOOKS THAN WE LOST....

BUT...

MY EMPLOYEES HELPED ME COUNT ALL THE BOOKS IN THE RESTAURANT.

AND THOSE, PLUS THE ONES YOU HAVE HERE, ADD UP TO MORE THAN 30,000 BOOKS!

30,000?!

YOU'RE RIGHT...

THAT **IS** A LOT OF BOOKS!

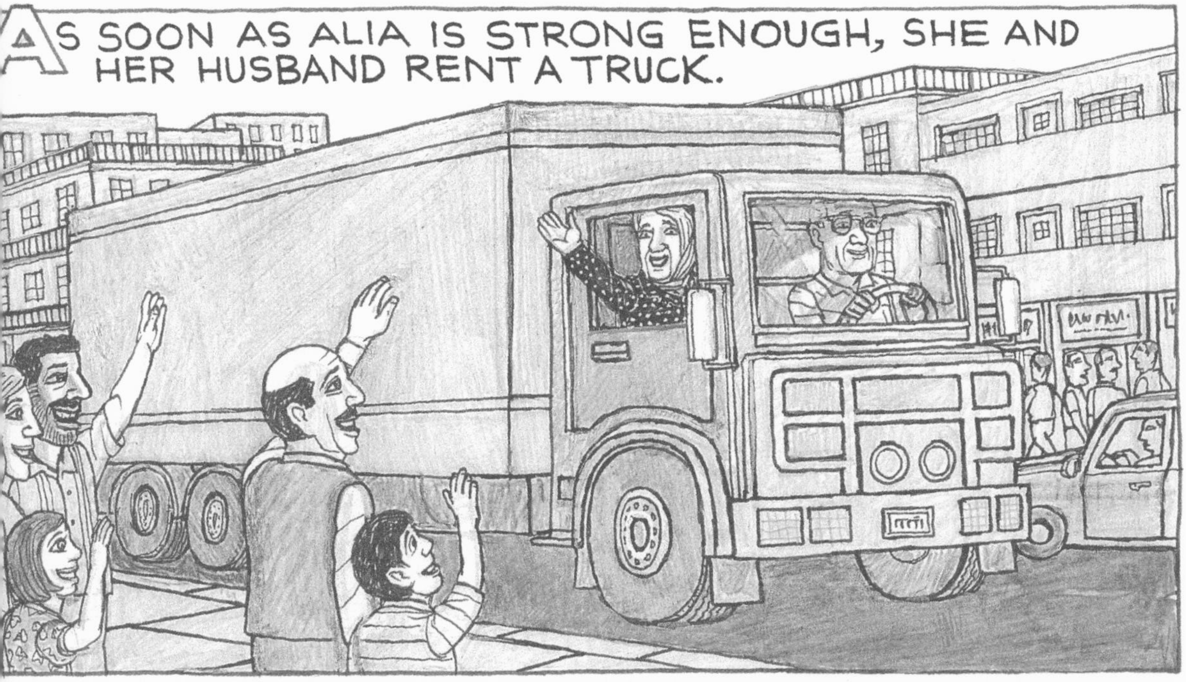
AS SOON AS ALIA IS STRONG ENOUGH, SHE AND HER HUSBAND RENT A TRUCK.

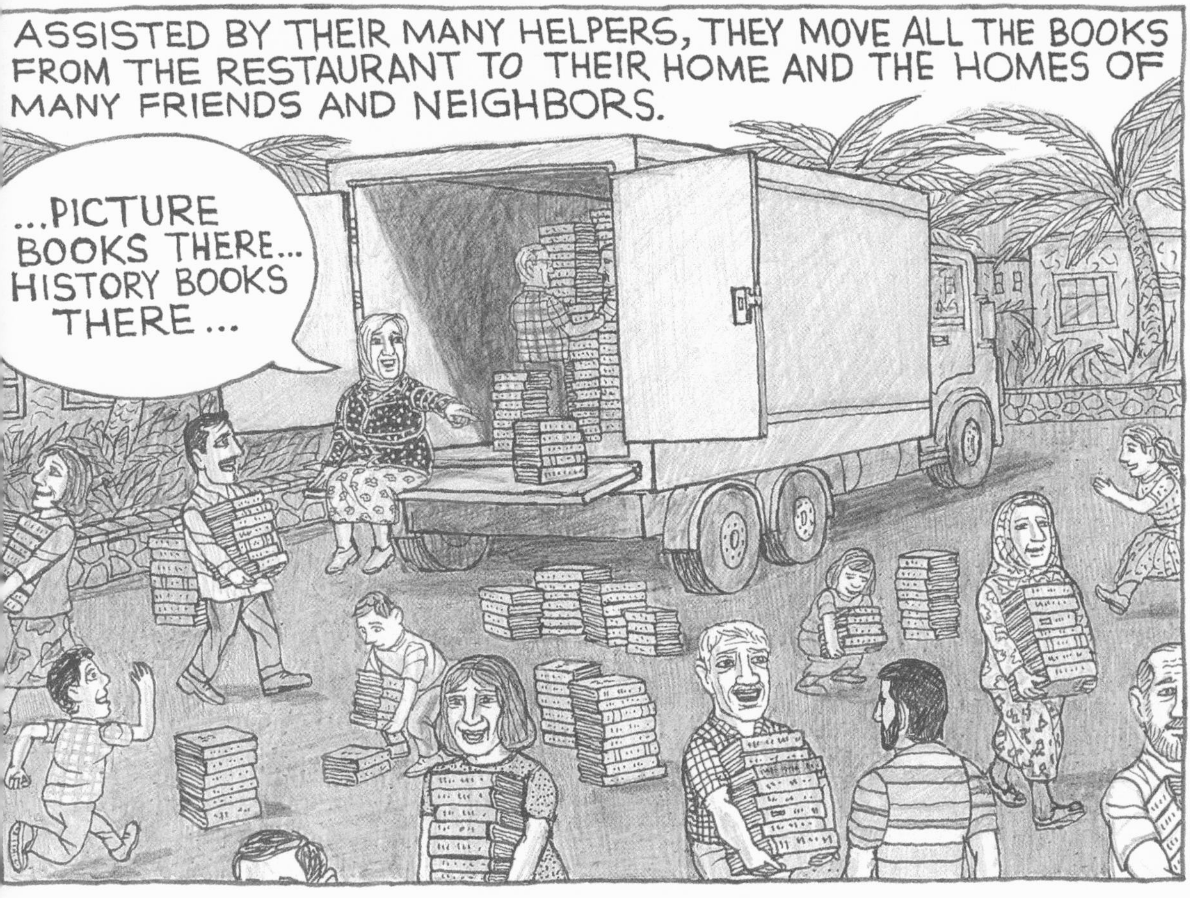
ASSISTED BY THEIR MANY HELPERS, THEY MOVE ALL THE BOOKS FROM THE RESTAURANT TO THEIR HOME AND THE HOMES OF MANY FRIENDS AND NEIGHBORS.
...PICTURE BOOKS THERE... HISTORY BOOKS THERE...

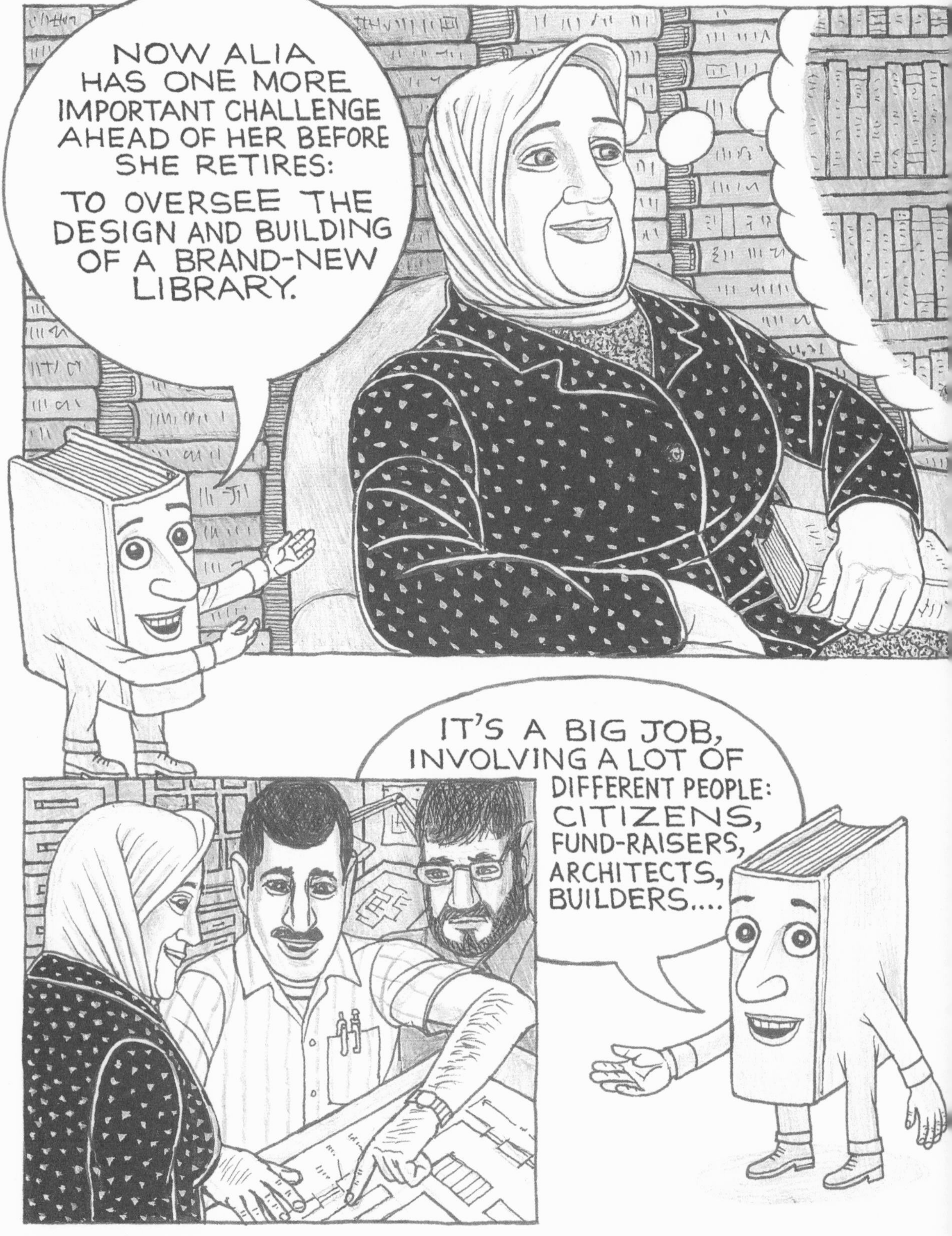
NOW ALIA HAS ONE MORE IMPORTANT CHALLENGE AHEAD OF HER BEFORE SHE RETIRES:
TO OVERSEE THE DESIGN AND BUILDING OF A BRAND-NEW LIBRARY.
IT'S A BIG JOB, INVOLVING A LOT OF DIFFERENT PEOPLE: CITIZENS, FUND-RAISERS, ARCHITECTS, BUILDERS....

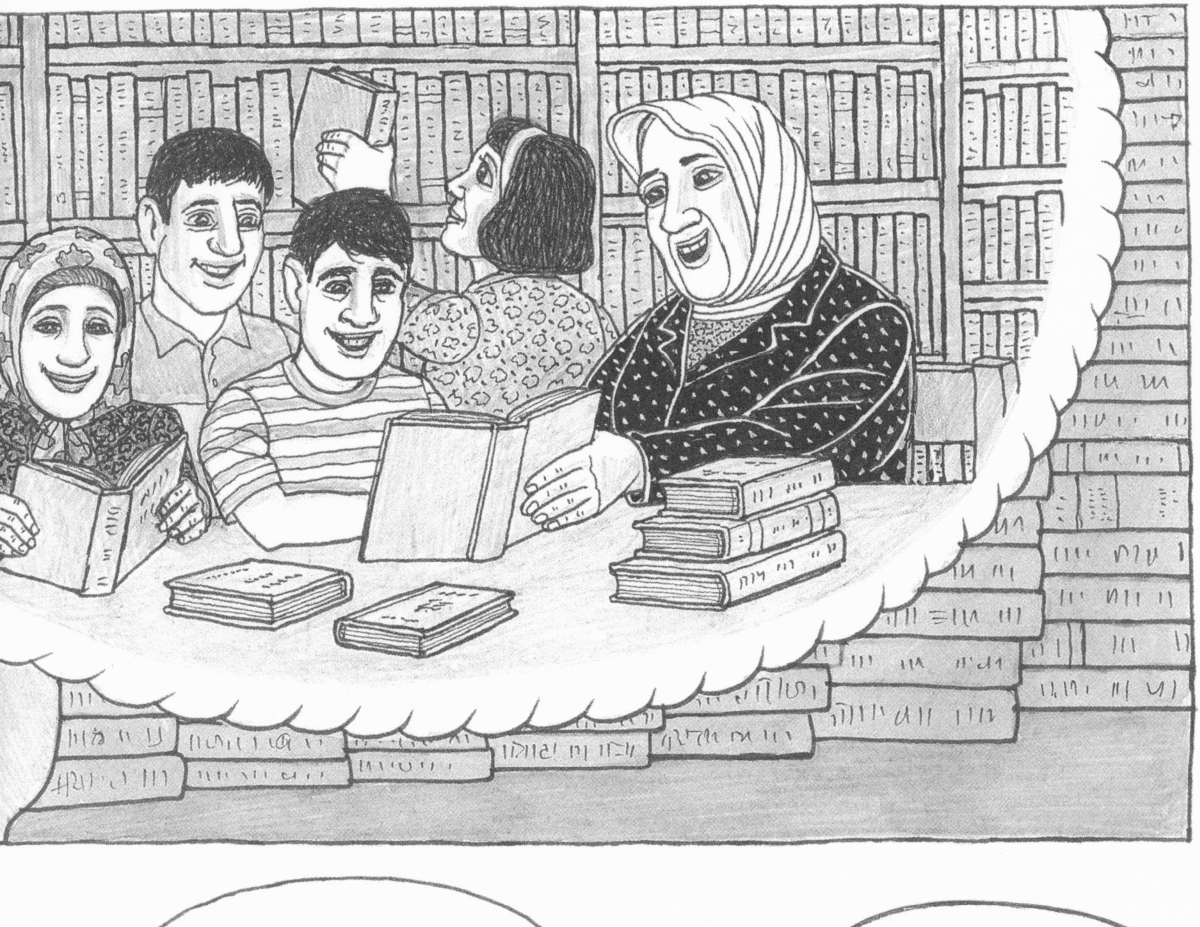

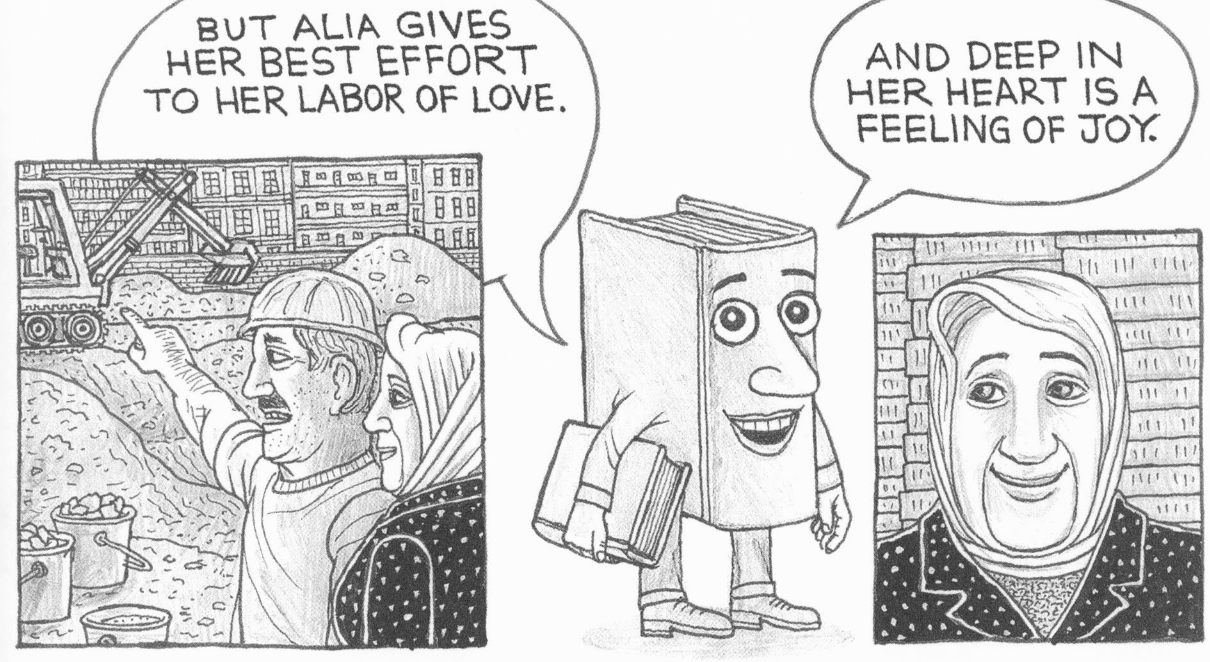
BUT ALIA GIVES HER BEST EFFORT TO HER LABOR OF LOVE.
AND DEEP IN HER HEART IS A FEELING OF JOY.

Alia's story is just the latest chapter in a long and fascinating history of libraries in Iraq and the Middle East. Here are some other stories you might not know....

- The land now called Iraq was actually the birthplace of all written language. Over five thousand years ago, in approximately 3500 BCE, the ancient Sumerians used split reeds from local marshes to make wedge-shaped markings on tablets of wet clay. When baked in the hot sun, the clay held permanent impressions; we now call these writings "cuneiform." Collections of these cuneiform tablets made up the world's first-ever libraries.

- The ancient Middle Eastern city of Ebla, in present-day Syria, had an extensive palace library, with over fifteen thousand clay tablets stored on wooden shelves. The entire city was destroyed by Akkadian invaders in 2250 BCE, but in 1980 an Italian archaeologist stumbled upon over two thousand of the clay documents still intact!

  How did these tablets survive over *four thousand years* of nature's wear and tear? After all, of over 500,000 texts held in the great Alexandrian Library of Egypt—built almost two thousand years after Ebla was destroyed—absolutely *nothing* remains. Both libraries were burned to the ground; what made such a difference at Ebla?

  The difference was that the manuscripts in Alexandria's library were papyrus—thin paper-like scrolls made from stripped, pressed plant stalks. Much like paper, papyrus burns very easily; the blaze that destroyed the Alexandrian Library in the late 200s CE turned its collection to ash. With Ebla's clay tablets, though, fire only baked them harder, making them even more durable. By burning Ebla down, its conquerors unknowingly *protected* the city's literature!

- The story of the burning of the great Baghdad library, the Nizamiyah, which made such an impression on Alia as a child, occurred during the Mongol invasion of 1258 CE. In only one week, Mongol leader Hulagu Khan ravaged almost all of the city's thirty-six public libraries. Legend has it that so many books were thrown into the Tigris River that the water ran blue from their ink.

- The Nizamiyah library was severely damaged but not destroyed by the Mongol invasions. In fact, it still stands today, the third-oldest library in the world. Alia's library, too, has survived hardships. Extensive repairs to the Basra Central Library are currently in progress. The library will undergo a complete refurbishment, paving the way for new services such as a computer lab with Internet access and a summer-school program for local children. Most importantly, though, the library will continue to house the tens of thousands of books Alia and her friends worked so hard to protect, the precious cultural history of Iraq.

To learn how you can help preserve libraries, please contact the International Relations Department of the American Library Association at 1-800-545-2433.

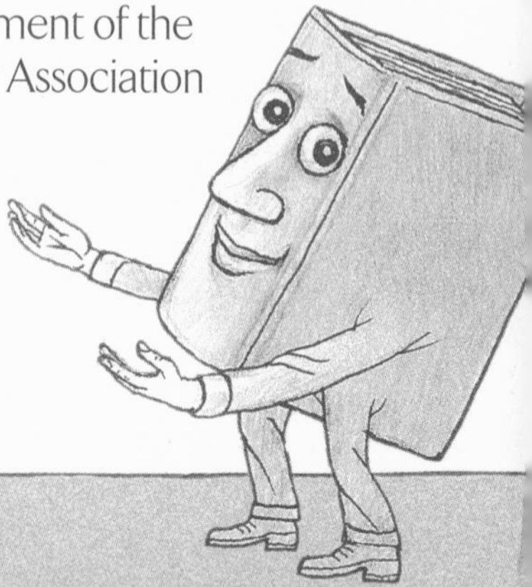